Piano • Vocal • Guitar

SECOND EDITION

THE BEST COUNTRY SONGS EVER

ISBN 978-0-7935-0636-1

HAL•LEONARD®
CORPORATION

7777 W. BLUEMOUND RD. P.O. BOX 13819 MILWAUKEE, WI 53213

Visit Hal Leonard Online at
www.halleonard.com

CONTENTS

AIN'T GOIN' DOWN
('Til the Sun Comes Up)

Words and Music by KIM WILLIAMS,
GARTH BROOKS and KENT BLAZY

Bright Country

mf

Six o'-clock on Fri - day eve-ning,
Nine o'-clock, the show is end-ing

Ma - ma does-n't know she's leav-ing 'til she hears the screen door slam-ming,
but the fun is just be-gin-ning. She knows he's an - tic - i - pat-ing,

back in bed be-fore the morn-ing."
danc-ing cheek to cheek.

They ain't go-ing down 'til the sun comes up, ain't

giv-ing in 'til they get e-nough.

Go-ing 'round the world in a

pick - up   truck. _____

no chord   To Coda ⊕   F   G

Ain't go - ing down 'til the sun comes up.

G

F

G

Ten 'til twelve is wine and danc - ing.   Mid - night starts the hard ro - manc - ing.
Six o' - clock on Sat - ur - day, her   folks don't know he's on his way. The

C

One o'-clock that truck is rock-ing.
stalls are clean, the hors-es fed. They

G

Two is com-ing, still no stop-ping.
say she's ground-ed 'til she's dead. Well,

D

Break to check the clock at three. They're
here he comes a-round the bend,

right at where they wan-ta be and
slow-ing down. She's jump-ing in.

G

four o'-clock get up and go-ing.
Hey, Mom, your daugh-ter's gone and

Five o'-clock that roost-er's crow-ing.
there they go a-gain. Hey. _____

Hey. _____

Instrumental solo each time

Solo ends   Yeah, they

Solo ends   They

sun comes up.   Yeah.

CODA

D.S. al Coda

D.S.S. and Fade

ALWAYS ON MY MIND

Words and Music by WAYNE THOMPSON,
MARK JAMES and JOHNNY CHRISTOPHER

Slow Ballad

May-be I did-n't treat you __ quite as good __ as I
May-be I did-n't hold you __ all those lone-ly, lone-ly

should have. May-be I did-n't love you __
times, __ and I guess I nev-er told you __

quite as of-ten as I could have. __
I'm so hap-py that you're mine. ____

(1.,3.) Lit-tle things should have
(2.) If I make you feel __

BEHIND CLOSED DOORS

Words and Music by
KENNY O'DELL

peo - ple like to talk, ___ Lord, don't they love ___ to talk.

But when they turn out the ___ lights, I

know she'll be leav - in' ___ with me; And when we get be-

hind closed ___ doors, then she lets her hair hang ___

Verse

2. (My) baby makes me smile, Lord, don't she make me smile.
   She's never far away or too tired to say I want you.
   She's always a lady, just like a lady should be
   But when they turn out the lights, she's still a baby to me. **(Chorus)**

BLUE

Words and Music by
BILL MACK

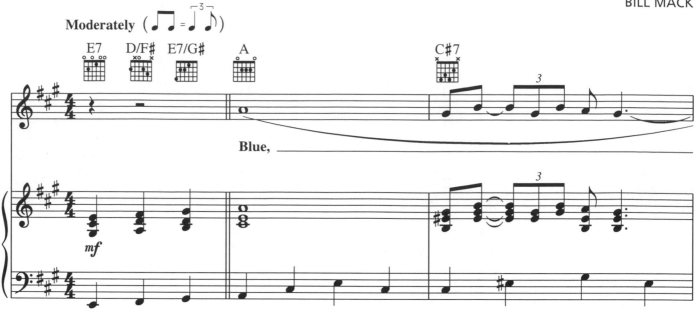

Blue,

— oh, so lone-some for __ you.   Why _ can't _ you be

blue _____ o - ver me?

BLUE BAYOU

Words and Music by ROY ORBISON
and JOE MELSON

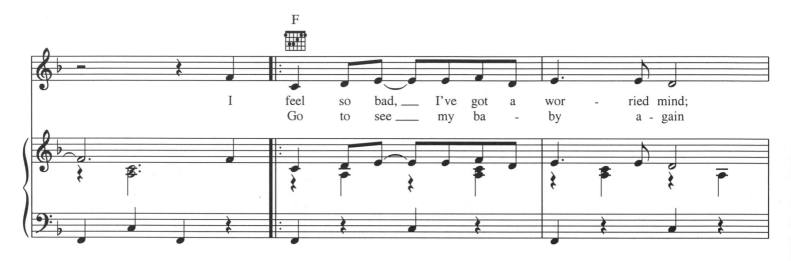

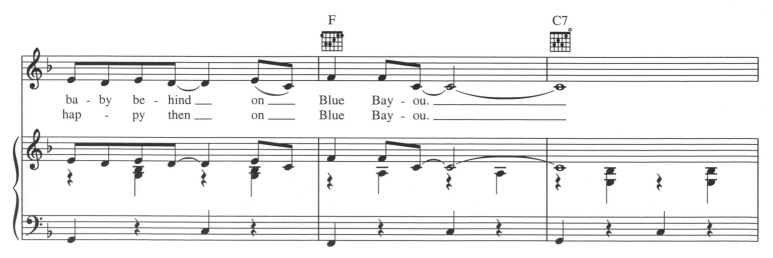

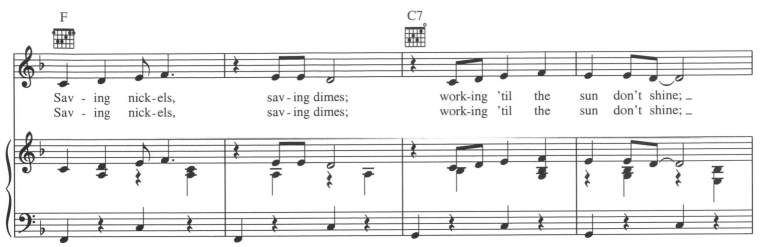

Sav - ing nick-els, sav-ing dimes; work-ing 'til the sun don't shine; __
Sav - ing nick-els, sav-ing dimes; work-ing 'til the sun don't shine; __

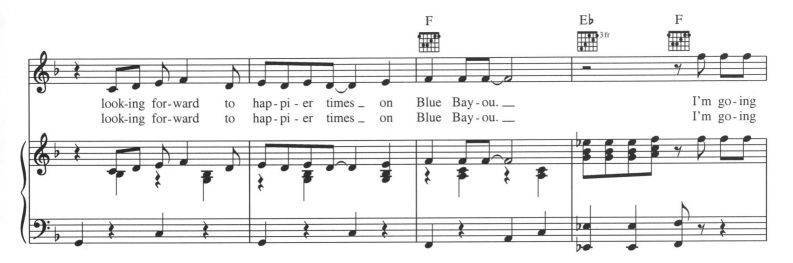

look-ing for-ward to hap-pi-er times __ on Blue Bay-ou. __ I'm go-ing
look-ing for-ward to hap-pi-er times __ on Blue Bay-ou. __ I'm go-ing

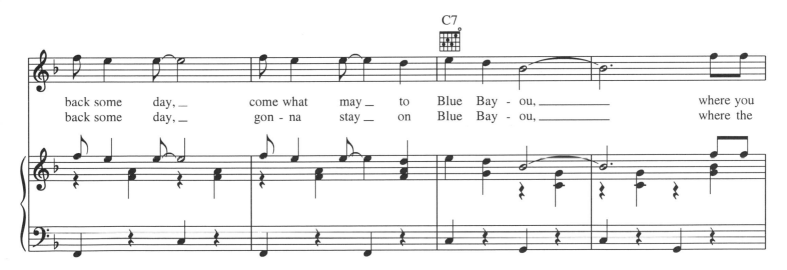

back some day, __ come what may __ to Blue Bay-ou, _____ where you
back some day, __ gon-na stay __ on Blue Bay-ou, _____ where the

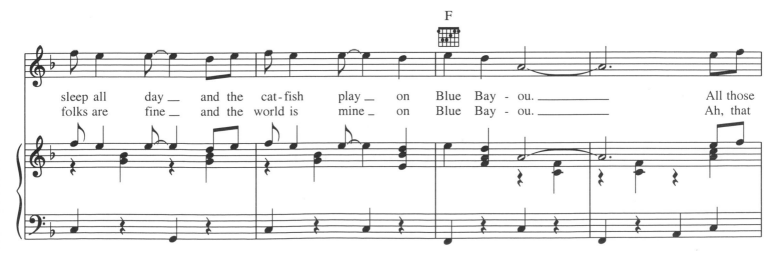

sleep all day __ and the cat-fish play __ on Blue Bay-ou. _____ All those
folks are fine __ and the world is mine __ on Blue Bay-ou. _____ Ah, that

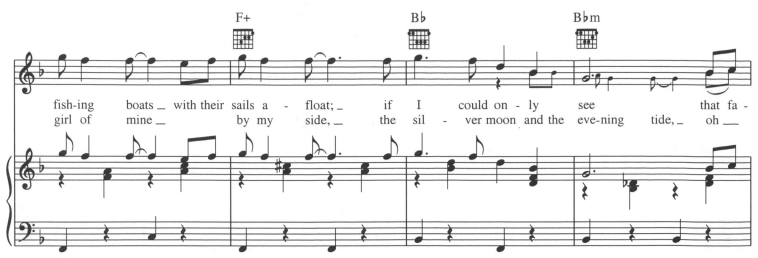

fish-ing boats _ with their sails a - float; _ if I could on - ly see that fa-
girl of mine _ by my side, _ the sil - ver moon and the eve-ning tide, _ oh _

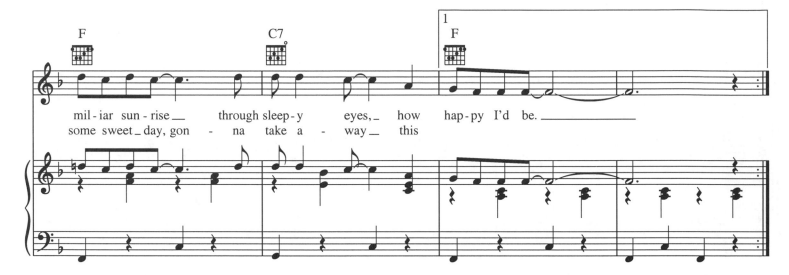

mil-iar sun-rise __ through sleep-y eyes,_ how hap-py I'd be. _____
some sweet _ day, gon - na take a - way _ this

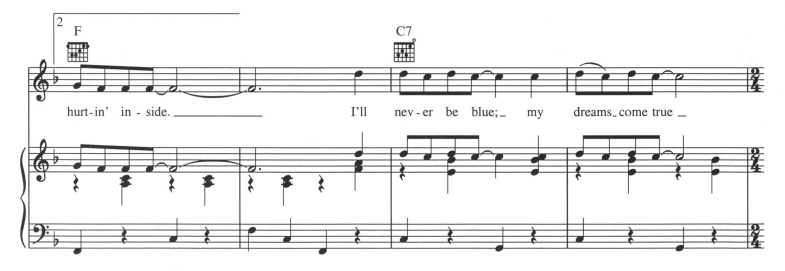

hurt-in' in - side. _____ I'll nev-er be blue;_ my dreams _ come true _

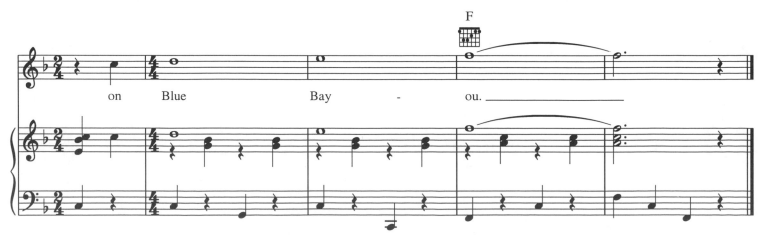

on Blue Bay - ou. _____

BLUE EYES CRYING IN THE RAIN

Words and Music by
FRED ROSE

Sad 2

F

In
Now the
my twi -
hair light
has glow
turned I
to see
sil her
- ver

blue
All eyes
my cry
life - ing
I've in
loved the
in

C7

F

rain
vain

As
I we
can

kissed good - bye and part - ed ____ I
see her star in heav - en ____

C7

knew we'd nev - er meet a - gain ____
blue eyes cry - ing in the rain ____

F   Bb

F   F7   Bb

Love is like a dy - ing
Some - day when we meet up

em - ber ____
yon - der ____

F

On - ly
We'll stroll

BUSTED

Words and Music by
HARLAN HOWARD

cow that went dry and a hen that won't lay, a
broth-er said, "There ain't a thing I can do; my
fields are all bare and the cot-ton won't grow.

big stack of bills that gets big-ger each day. The
wife and my kids are all down with the flu; and
Me and my fam-'ly got to pack up and go, but

coun-ty's gon-na haul my be-long-ings a-way 'cause I'm bust-ed. __
I was just think-ing a-bout call-ing on you! And I'm bust-ed." __
I'll make a liv-ing just where I don't know 'cause I'm bust-ed. __

Well,

Repeat and Fade

(Spoken:) I'm broke!   No bread! I mean like nothin' Forget it!

BY THE TIME I GET TO PHOENIX

Words and Music by
JIMMY WEBB

30

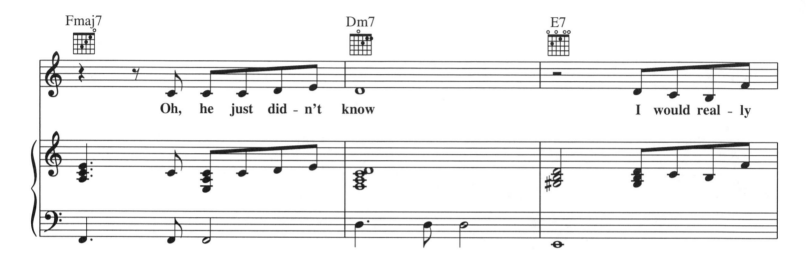

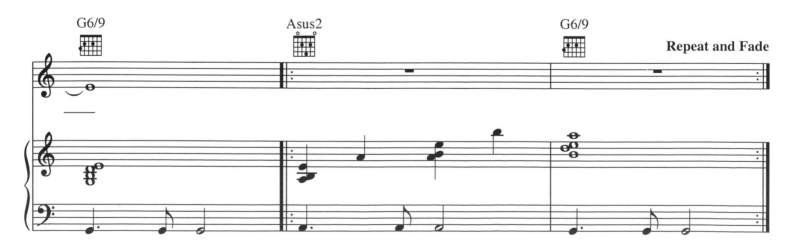

COULD I HAVE THIS DANCE

Words and Music by WAYLAND HOLYFIELD
and BOB HOUSE

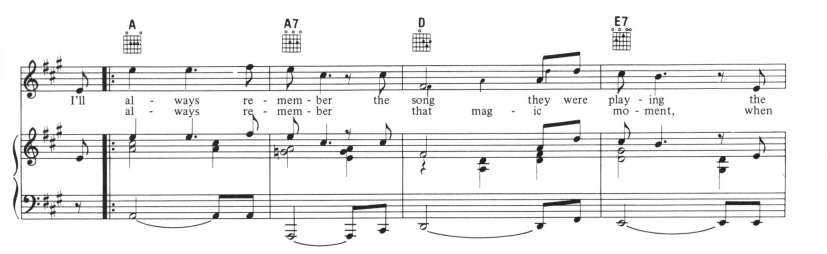

I'll al - ways re - mem - ber the song they were play - ing, the
al - ways re - mem - ber that mag - ic mo - ment, when

first time   we danced and I knew.
I held   you close to me.

As we
As

swayed to the mu- sic____ and held to each oth- er,____
we moved to -geth- er,____ I knew for - ev - er____

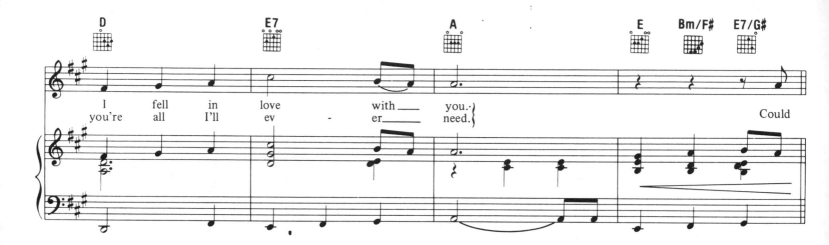

I fell in love____ with____ you.
you're all I'll love ev - er____ need.

Could

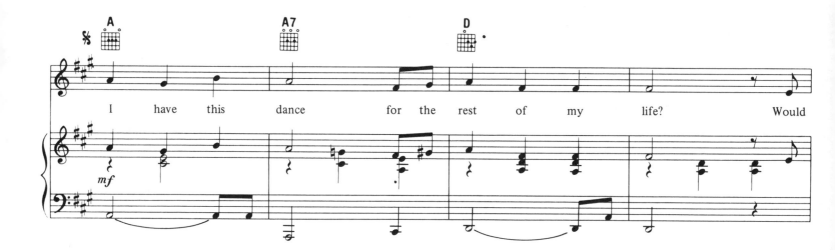

I have this dance for the rest of my life? Would

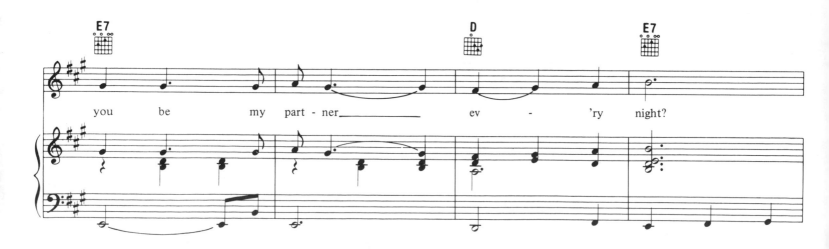

you be my part - ner____ ev - 'ry night?

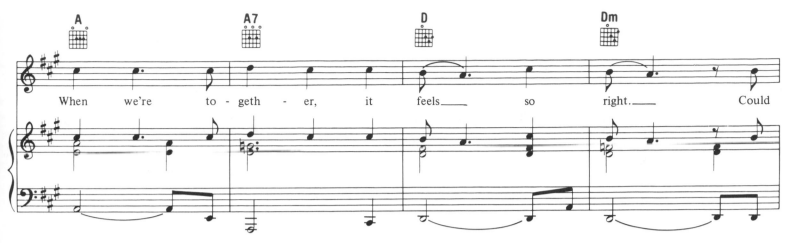

When we're to-geth - er, it feels____ so right.____ Could

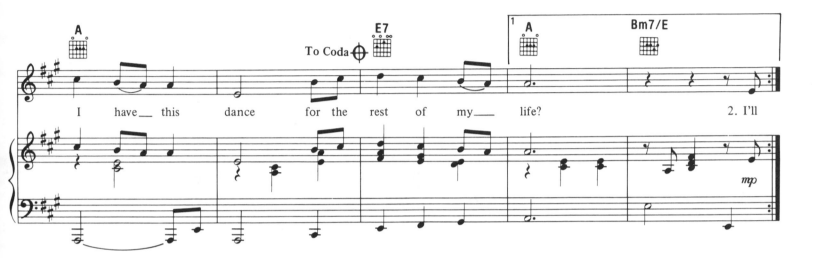

I have____ this dance for the rest of my____ life? 2. I'll

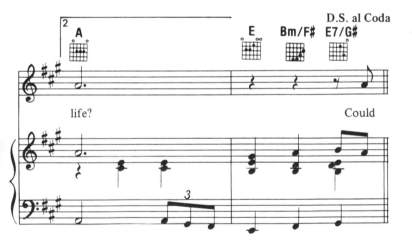

life? Could

rest of my____

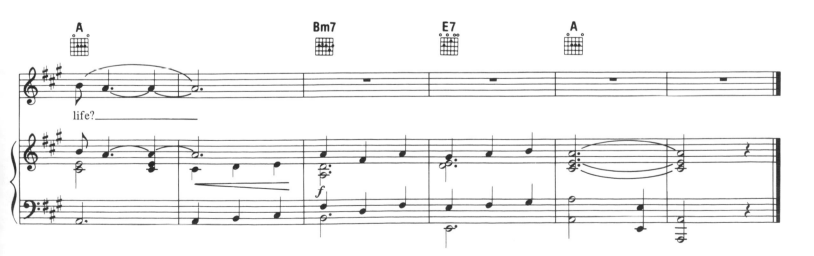

life?____

CRAZY

Words and Music by
WILLIE NELSON

I knew _____ you'd love me as long as you
want - ed, _____ and then some - day __ you'd
leave me for some - bod - y new.
Wor - ry, __ why do I let my - self wor - ry, _____

CRYING

Words and Music by ROY ORBISON
and JOE MELSON

Moderately slow, with feeling

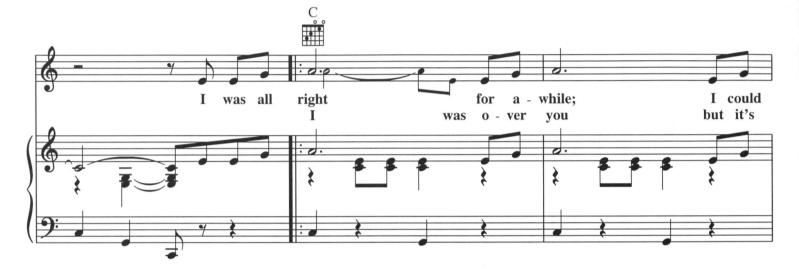

I was all right for a - while; I could
I was o - ver you but it's

smile for a - while, but I saw you last night; you held my
true, so true, I love you e - ven more than I

hand so tight, as you stopped to say, "Hel - lo." Oh, you
did be - fore, but dar - ling, what can I do? For you

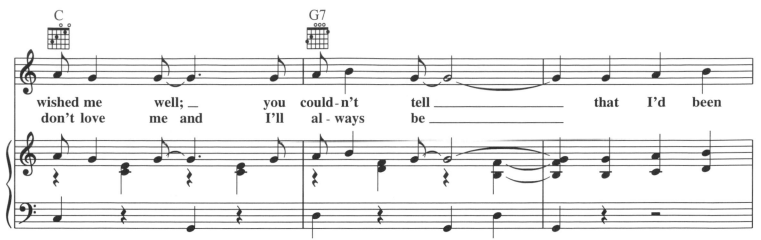

wished me well; __ you could-n't tell _____ that I'd been
don't love me and I'll al - ways be _____

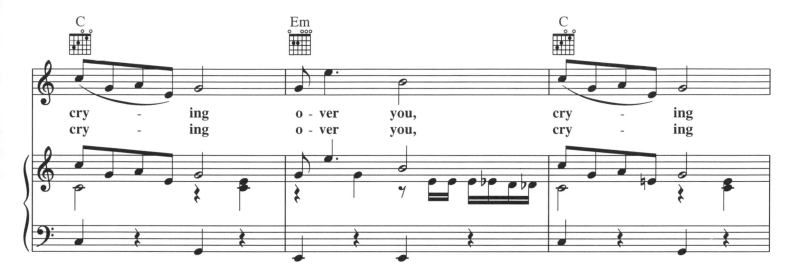

cry - ing o - ver you, cry - ing
cry - ing o - ver you, cry - ing

o - ver you. When you said, "So
o - ver you. Yes, now you're __

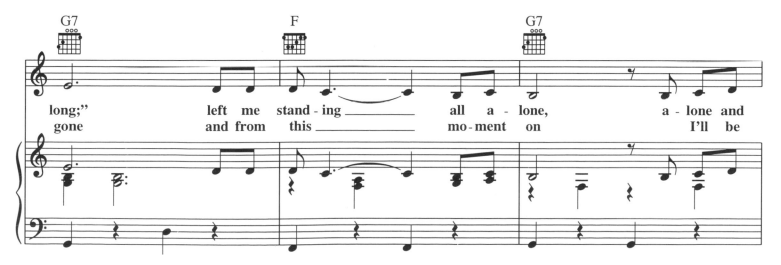

long;" left me stand - ing _____ all a - lone, a - lone and
gone and from this _____ mo - ment on I'll be

CRYING IN THE CHAPEL

Words and Music by
ARTIE GLENN

Slowly, with expression

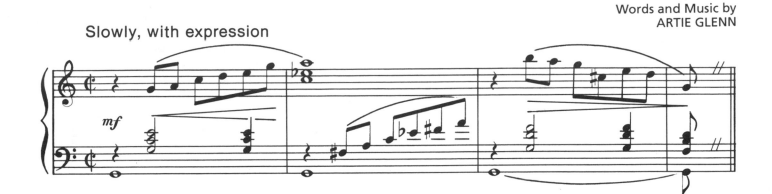

Chorus

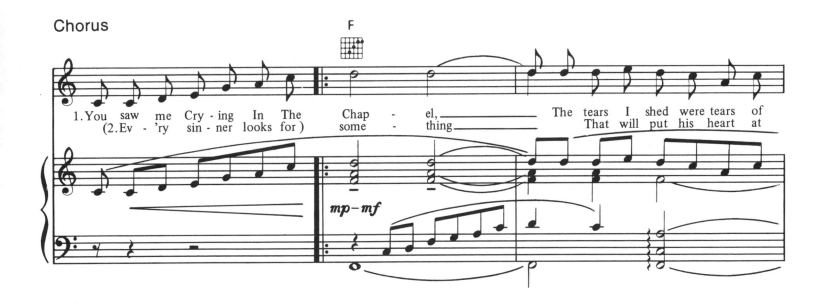

1. You saw me Cry-ing In The Chap-el, some-thing _____ The tears I shed were tears of
(2. Ev-'ry sin-ner looks for) That will put his heart at

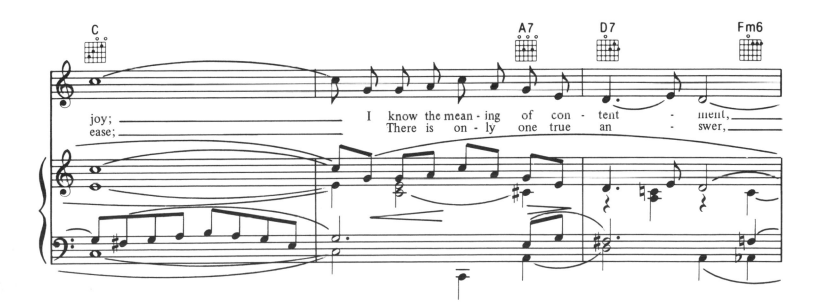

joy; _____ I know the mean-ing of con-tent-ment, _____
ease; _____ There is on-ly one true an-swer, _____

DADDY SANG BASS

Words and Music by
CARL PERKINS

Moderately fast

I re-mem-ber when I was a lad, times were hard and things were bad; But there's a

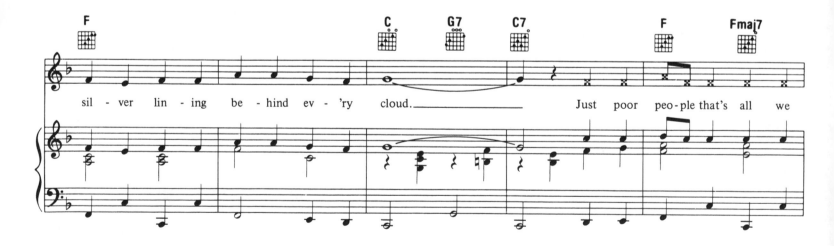

sil-ver lin-ing be-hind ev-'ry cloud._____ Just poor peo-ple that's all we

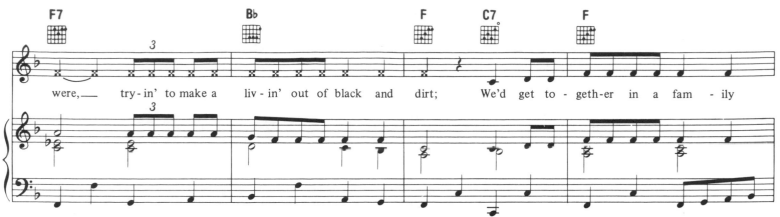

were,___ try-in' to make a liv-in' out of black and dirt; We'd get to-geth-er in a fam-ily

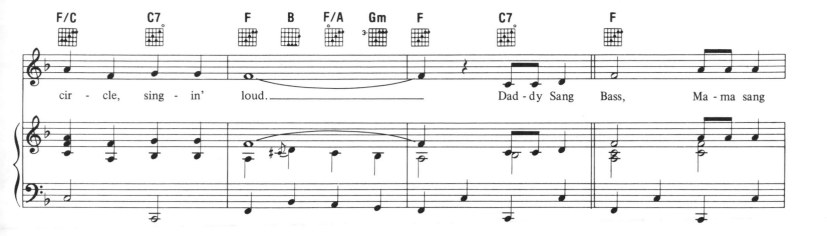

cir-cle, sing-in' loud._____ Dad-dy Sang Bass, Ma-ma sang

ten-or me and lit-tle bro-ther would join right in there Sing-in' seems to help a trou-bled

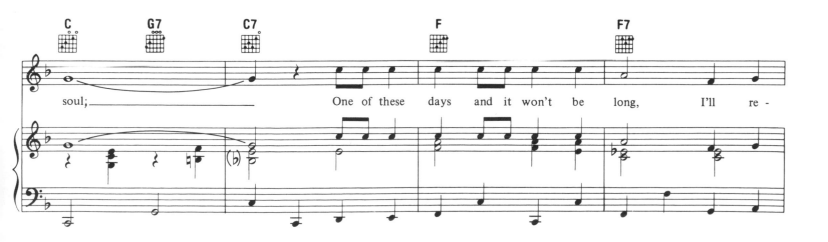

soul;_____ One of these days and it won't be long, I'll re-

join them in a song; I'm gon-na join the fam-i-ly cir-cle at the

throne;_____ No, the cir - cle won't be

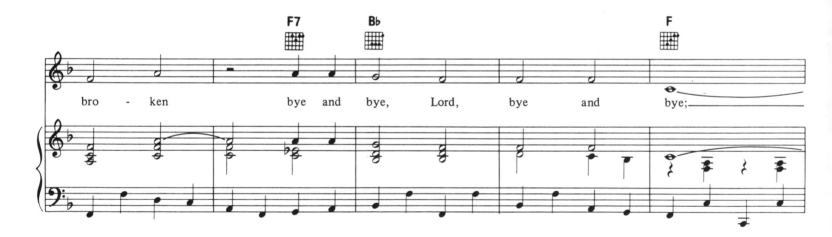

bro - ken bye and bye, Lord, bye and bye;_____

D.S. and Fade

_____ Dad-dy-'ll sing bass, Ma-ma-'ll sing ten - or, me and lit - tle bro-ther will join right

DADDY'S HANDS

Words and Music by
HOLLY DUNN

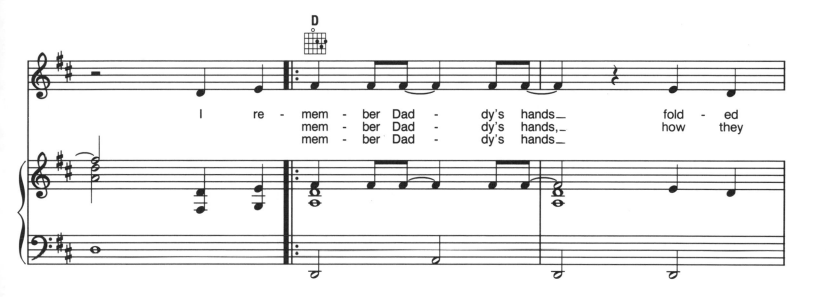

I re- mem- ber Dad - dy's hands____ fold - ed
mem - ber Dad - dy's hands,____ how they
mem - ber Dad - dy's hands____

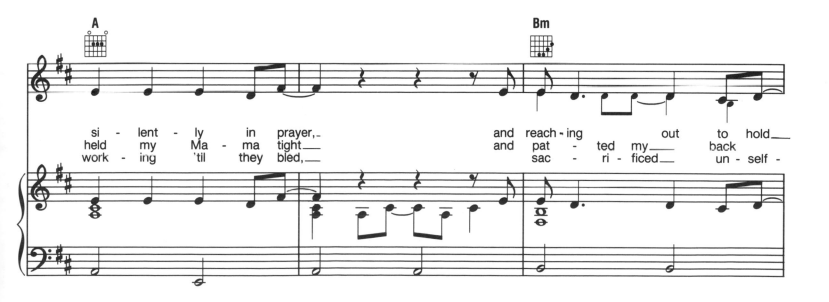

si - lent - ly in prayer,____ and reach- ing out to hold____
held my Ma- ma tight____ and pat - ted my____ back
work - ing 'til they bled,____ sac - ri - ficed un- self -

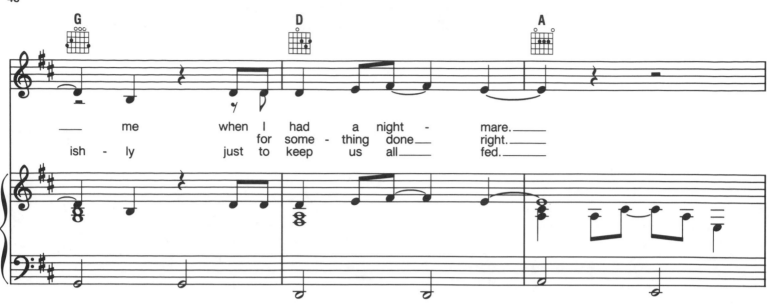

me when I had a night - mare.___
ish - ly just to keep us all___ fed.___

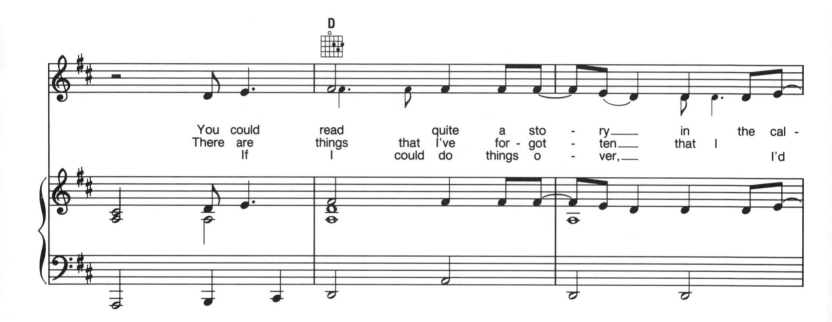

You could read quite a sto - ry___ in the cal -
There are things that I've for - got - ten___ that I
If I could do things o - ver,___ I'd

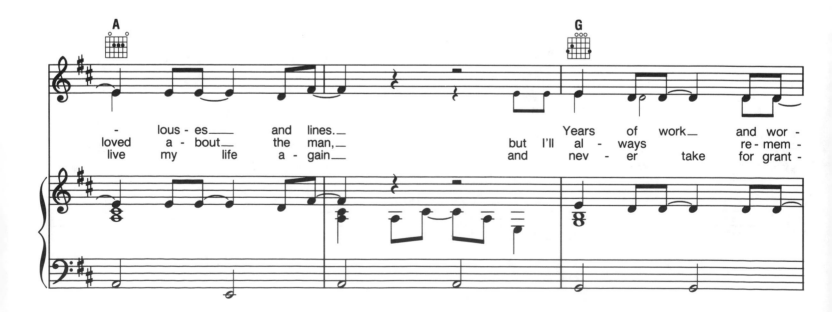

- lous - es___ and lines.___ Years of work___ and wor -
loved a - bout___ the man,___ but I'll al - ways re - mem -
live my life a - gain___ and nev - er take for grant -

hands weren't al - ways gen - tle but I've come to un - der - stand,_____

____ there was al - ways love in Dad - dy's hands.

I re - Dad - dy's

love_____

in Dad - dy's

hands.

EASY COME, EASY GO

Words and Music by DEAN DILLON
and AARON BARKER

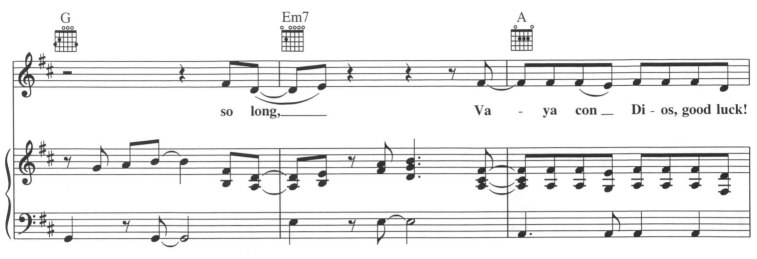

so long,____ Va - ya con ___ Di - os, good luck!

Wish you well, take it slow,____ eas - y come,_

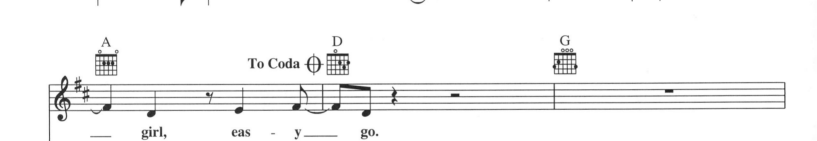

___ girl, eas - y ___ go.

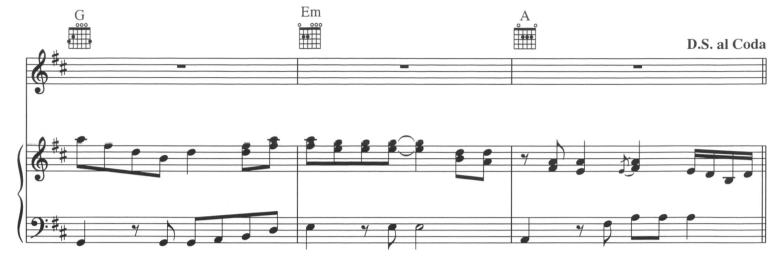

D.S. al Coda

CODA

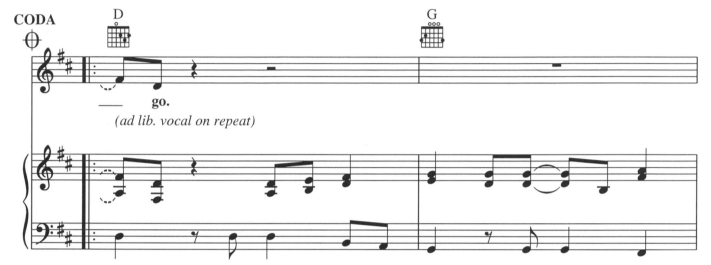

__ go.

(ad lib. vocal on repeat)

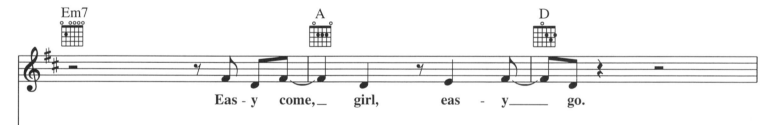

Eas - y come,_ girl, eas - y____ go.

Repeat ad lib. and Fade

Vay - a con Di - os, good luck!

EIGHTEEN WHEELS AND A DOZEN ROSES

Words and Music by GENE NELSON
and PAUL NELSON

life with the one that he____ loves.

They'll loves.

Eigh - teen

Repeat and fade

Instrumental - to fade

wheels _____ and a doz - en ros - es, ten more

miles _____ on his four - day run. A few more

songs _____ from the all night rad - i - o then he'll

spend the rest of his life with the one that he loves.

ELVIRA

Words and Music by
DALLAS FRAZIER

Verse 2. Tonight I'm gonna meet her
At the hungry house cafe
And I'm gonna give her all the love I can
She's gonna jump and holler
'Cause I saved up my last two dollar
And we're gonna search and find that preacher man
Chorus

FOR THE GOOD TIMES

Words and Music by
KRIS KRISTOFFERSON

Slowly

Gm — **Gm7** — **C7** — **F** — **F6**

Don't look so sad; _____ I know it's o - ver; _____
long; _____ you'll find an - oth - er; _____

Fmaj7 — **F6** — **Gm** — **Gm7** — **C7** — **C7sus**

But life goes on _____ and this old world _____ will keep on
And I'll be on here _____ if you should find _____ you ev - er

F — **F6** — **Fmaj7** — **F** — **F7** — **Bb**

turn - ing. _____ Let's just be glad _____ we had some
need me. _____ Don't say a word _____ a - bout to -

FOREVER AND EVER, AMEN

Words and Music by DON SCHLITZ
and PAUL OVERSTREET

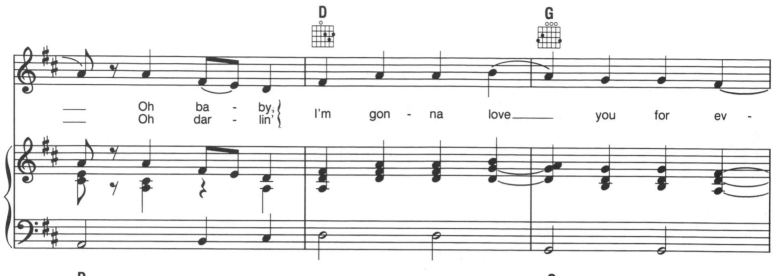

Oh ba - by,   I'm gon - na love_____ you for ev -
Oh dar - lin'

- er,_____ for - ev - er and ev -

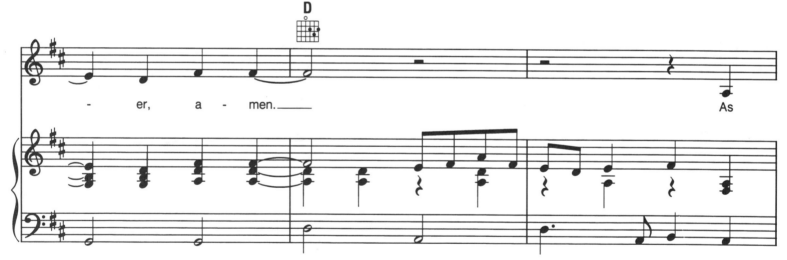

- er, a - men._____ As

long as old men_____ sit and talk a - bout_____ the wea -

FRIENDS IN LOW PLACES

Words and Music by DEWAYNE BLACKWELL
and EARL BUD LEE

last one to show; ___ I was the last ___ one you thought you'd see
just say good - night ___ and I'll show ___ my - self ___ to the door. ___

there. ___ And I saw the sur - prise ___ and the
Hey, I did - n't mean ___ to

B♭dim7

Bm7

fear in his eyes ___ when I took his glass ___ of cham - pagne. ___
cause a big scene, ___ just give me an ho - ur and

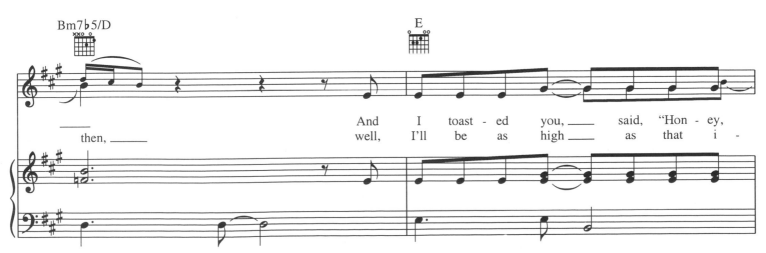

Bm7♭5/D

E

then, ___
well, I'll be as high ___ as that i -

And I toast - ed you, ___ said, "Hon - ey,

we may be through, _____ but you'll nev - er hear ____ me com - plain."
- vo - ry tow - er that you're liv - in' in. ___

A

'Cause I've got friends __ in low plac - es where the

whis - key ____ drowns ___ and the beer ____ chas - es my blues ___

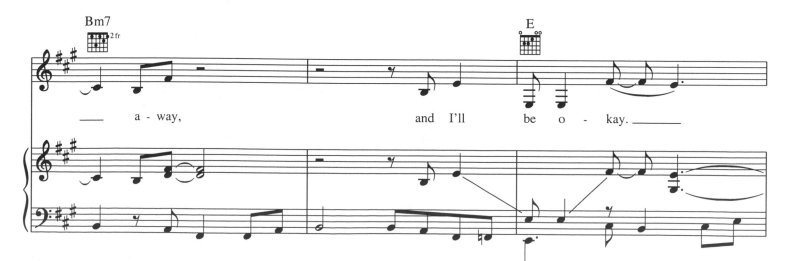

Bm7

E

___ a - way, and I'll be o - kay. ___

Yeah, I'm not big ___ on so - cial grac - es. Think I'll

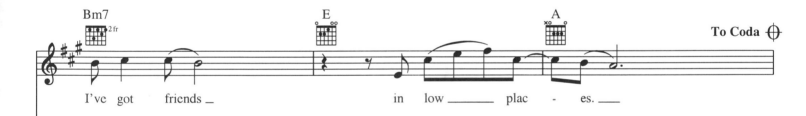

slip on ___ down ___ to the o - a - sis. Oh, ___

I've got friends _ in low ___ plac - es. _

To Coda ⊕

Well, I

I've got friends in low plac - es where the

whis - key ___ drowns ___ and the beer ___ chas - es my blues ___

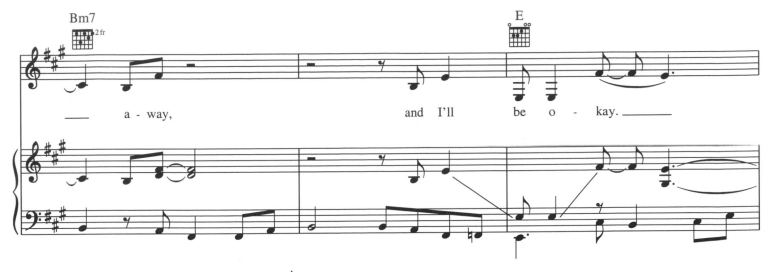

a - way, and I'll be o - kay.

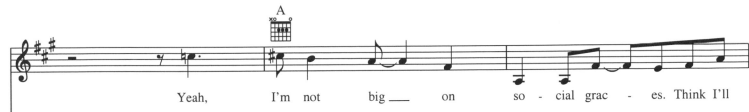

Yeah, I'm not big ___ on so - cial grac - es. Think I'll

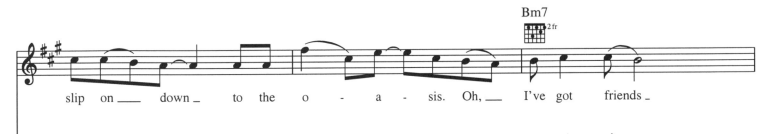

slip on ___ down ___ to the o - a - sis. Oh, ___ I've got friends ___

Repeat and Fade   **Optional Ending**

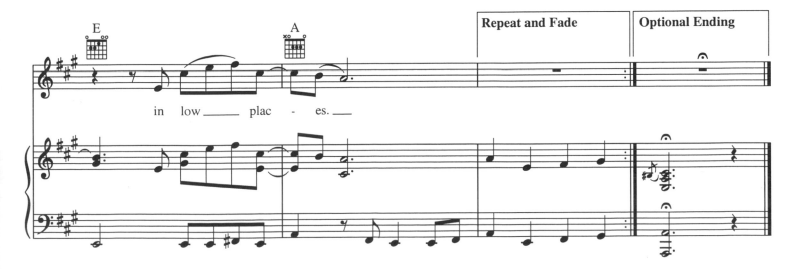

in low ___ plac - es. ___

FUNNY HOW TIME SLIPS AWAY

Words and Music by
WILLIE NELSON

GOD BLESS THE U.S.A.

Words and Music by
LEE GREENWOOD

Slowly

Verse

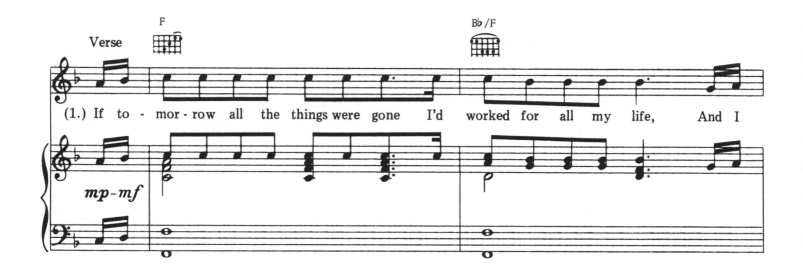

(1.) If to-mor-row all the things were gone I'd worked for all my life, And I

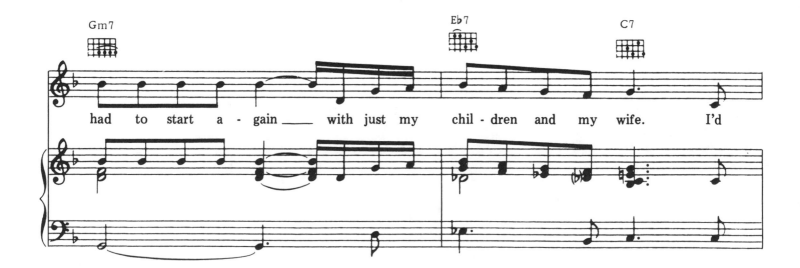

had to start a-gain ___ with just my chil-dren and my wife. I'd

MCA Music Publishing

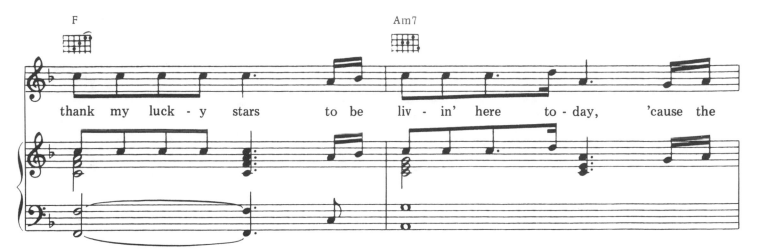

thank my luck - y stars to be liv - in' here to - day, 'cause the

flag still stands for free - dom and they can't take that a - way._____ And I'm

Chorus

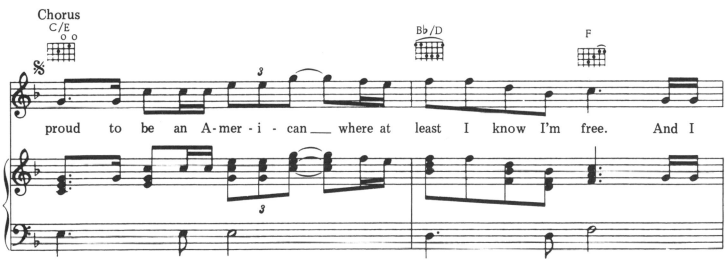

proud to be an A - mer - i - can___ where at least I know I'm free. And I

won't for - get the men who died, who gave that right to me. And I'd glad - ly

stand up;   next   to   you   and de - fend   her   still   to - day.   'Cause there

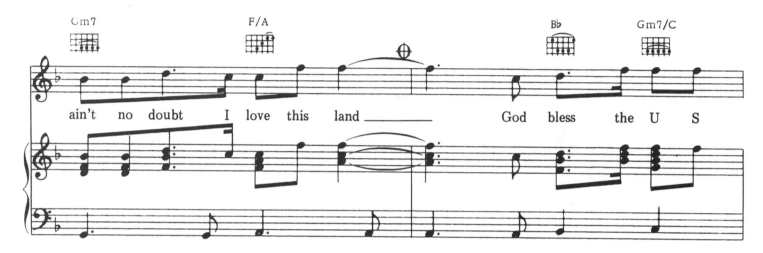

ain't   no   doubt   I   love   this   land _____   God   bless   the   U   S

A   (2.) From the

Verse

lakes   of   Min - ne - so - ta,   to   the   hills   of   Ten - nes - see, __   a -

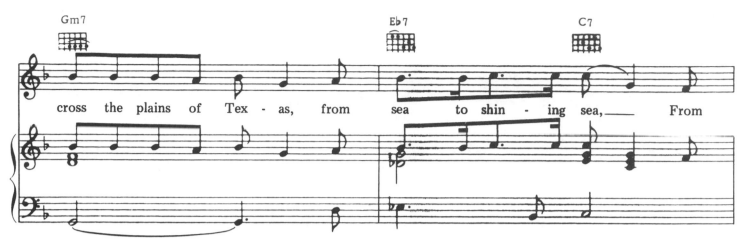

cross the plains of Tex - as, from sea to shin - ing sea,____ From

De - troit down to Hous - ton and New York to L A Well, there's

D. S. al Coda

pride in ev - 'ry A - mer - i - can heart, and it's time to stand and say____ That I'm

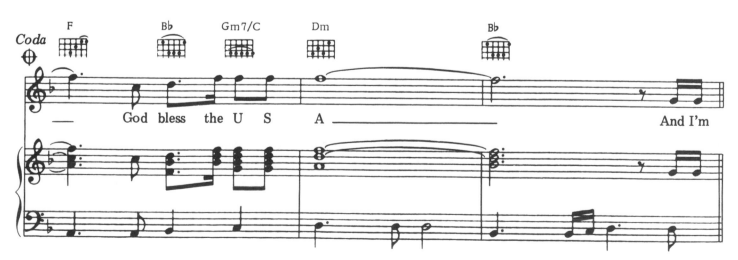

Coda

____ God bless the U S A ____ And I'm

Chorus

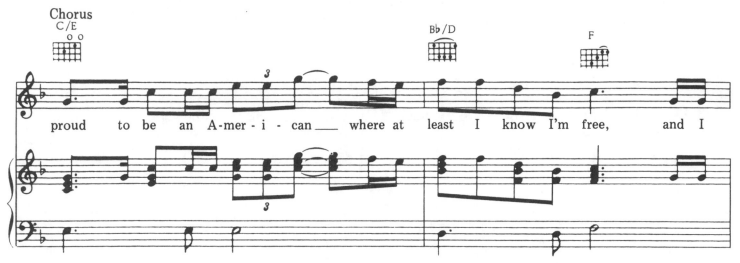

proud to be an A-mer-i-can____ where at least I know I'm free, and I

won't for-get the men who died, who gave that right to me. And I'd glad-ly

stand up next to you, and de-fend her still to-day. 'Cause there

ain't no doubt I love this land____ God bless the U S A____

GREEN GREEN GRASS OF HOME

Words and Music by
CURLY PUTMAN

Moderately Slow

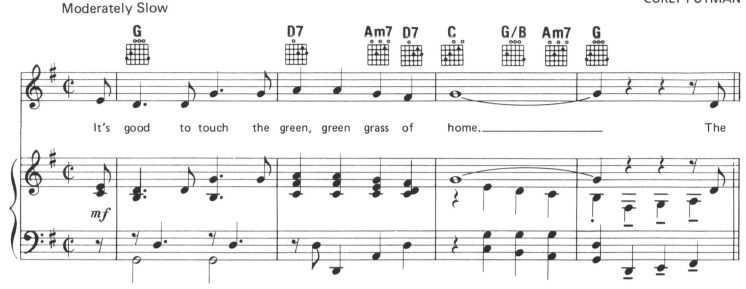

It's good to touch the green, green grass of home._____ The

old home town__ looks the same as I step down from the
old house is still stand-ing tho' the paint is cracked and

(Spoken:) Then I awake and look around me at four gray walls

train,_____ and there to meet me is my ma - ma__ and
dry,_____ and there's that old oak tree that I used__ to

that surround me and I realize that I was only dreaming.

A GOOD HEARTED WOMAN

Words and Music by WAYLON JENNINGS
and WILLIE NELSON

Lyrics:

A long time forgotten, are dreams that just
He likes the night life, the bright lights and

fell by the way.
good-timin' friends.

And the good life he promised ain't what she's
When the party's all over she'll welcome

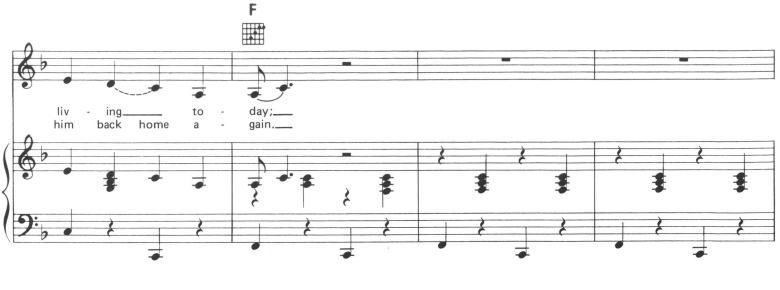

good times to___ come.
good - tim - in'___ man.

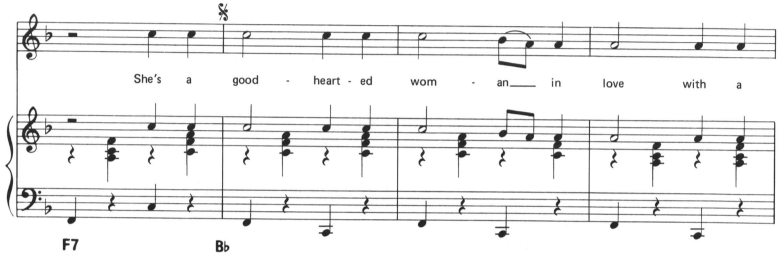

She's a good - heart - ed wom - an___ in love with a

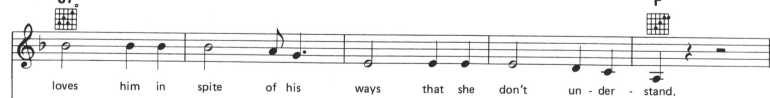

good - tim - in' man. She

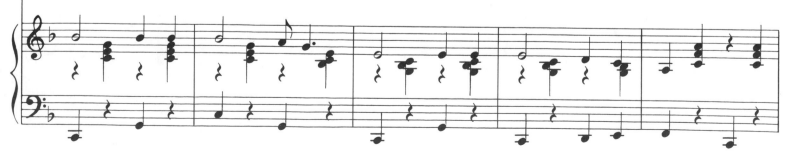

loves him in spite of his ways that she don't un - der - stand.

Through tear - drops and laugh - ter, they'll

F7 **Bb**

pass through this world _ hand - in - hand,

C7

a good - heart - ed wom - an lov - in' her good - tim - in'

F

man.

1.

2.

D.S. and Fade

She's a

GRANDPA
(Tell Me 'Bout the Good Old Days)

Words and Music by
JAMIE O'HARA

Medium Slow Country

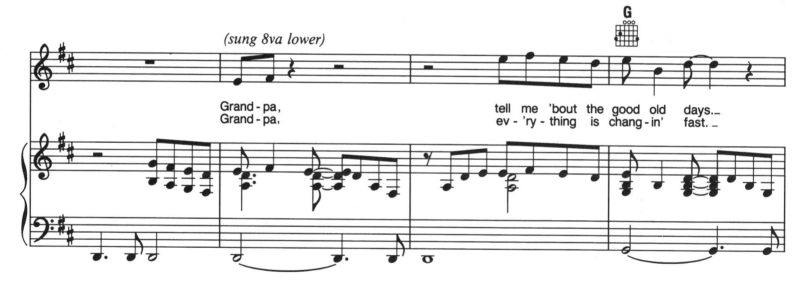

(sung 8va lower)

Grand-pa,   tell me 'bout the good old days.
Grand-pa,   ev-'ry-thing is chang-in' fast.

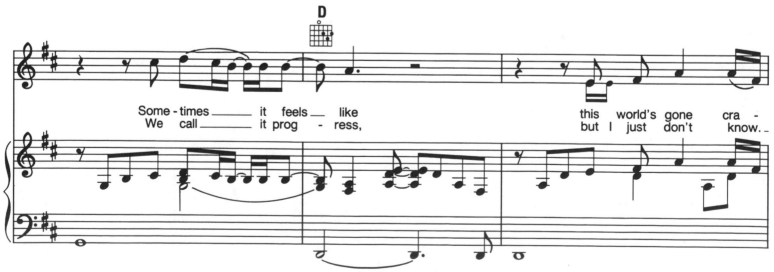

Some-times _____ it feels _____ like   this world's gone cra-
We call _____ it prog -ress,   but I just don't know. _____

HARPER VALLEY P.T.A.

Words and Music by
TOM T. HALL

Moderately (with a heavy beat)

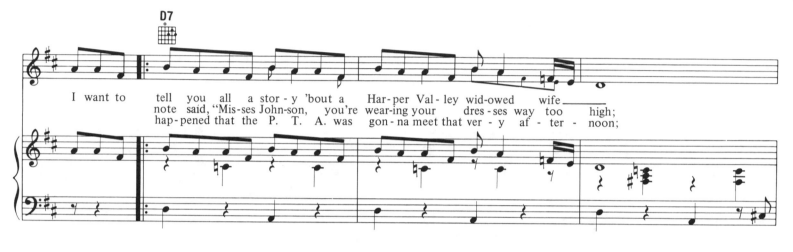

I want to tell you all a sto-ry 'bout a Har-per Val-ley wid-owed wife___
note said, "Mis-ses John-son, you're wear-ing your dres-ses way too high;
hap-pened that the P. T. A. was gon-na meet that ver - y af-ter-noon;

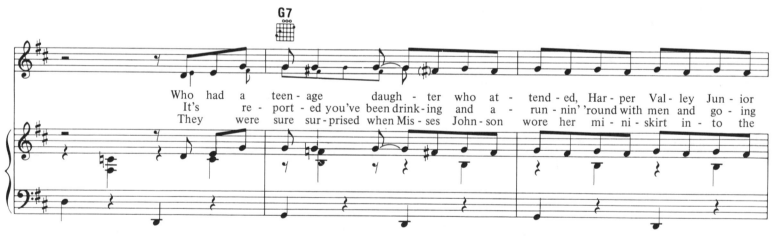

Who had a teen-age daugh-ter who at - tend-ed, Har-per Val-ley Jun-ior
It's re - port-ed you've been drink-ing and a - run-nin' 'round with men and go - ing
They were sure sur-prised when Mis-ses John-son wore her mi - ni-skirt in-to the

high. Well her daugh-ter came home___ one af-ter-
wild: And we don't be-lieve you ought to be a-
room. And as she walked up to the black-board, I

noon, and did-n't ev-en stop to play;
bring-ing up your lit-tle girl this way."
still re-call the words she had to say;

She said, "Mom, I got a note here from the
It was signed by the sec-re-tar-y,
She said, "I'd like to ad-dress this meet-ing

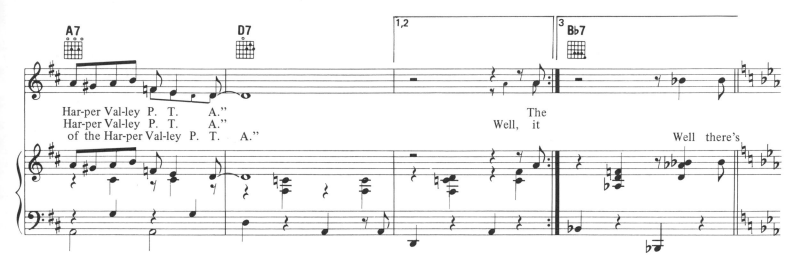

Har-per Val-ley P. T. A."
Har-per Val-ley P. T. A."
of the Har-per Val-ley P. T. A."

The
Well, it
Well there's

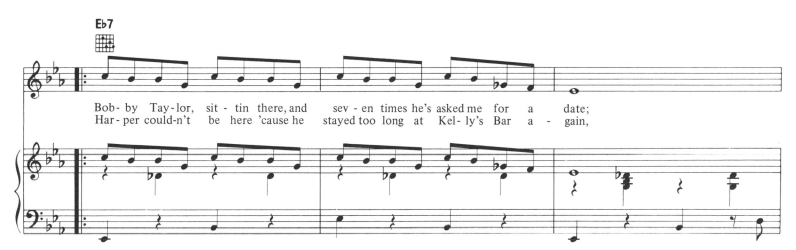

Bob-by Tay-lor, sit-tin there, and sev-en times he's asked me for a date;
Har-per could-n't be here 'cause he stayed too long at Kel-ly's Bar a-gain,

Miss-es Tay-lor sure seems to use a lot of ice when ev-er he's a-
And if you smell Shir-ley Tomp-son's breath, you'll find she's had a lit-tle nip of

HELLO WALLS

Words and Music by
WILLIE NELSON

Guitar Tacet

ceil - ing,_____ I'm gon - na stare at you a - while you know I

can't sleep, so won't you bear with me a - while? We must

all pull to - geth - er or else I'll lose my mind, 'cause I've got a

feel - in' she'll be gone a long, long time._____

HE STOPPED LOVING HER TODAY

Words and Music by BOBBY BRADDOCK
and CURLY PUTMAN

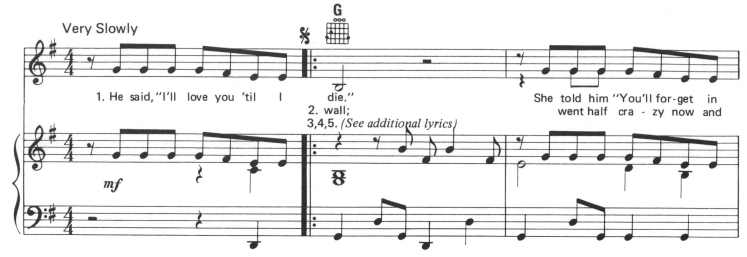

1. He said, "I'll love you 'til I die."
2. wall;
3,4,5. (See additional lyrics)

She told him "You'll for-get in
went half cra - zy now and

time."
then,

As the years went slow - ly by
but he still loved her through it all,

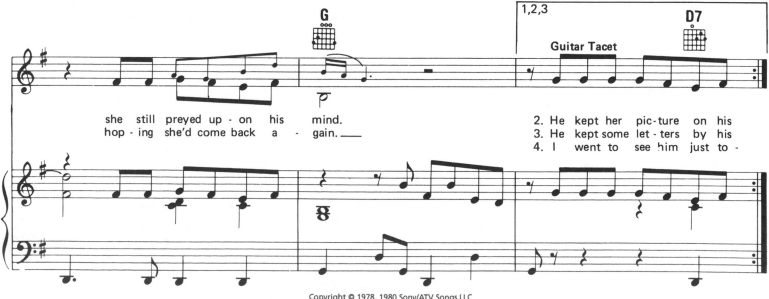

she still preyed up - on his mind.
hop - ing she'd come back a - gain. ___

2. He kept her pic - ture on his
3. He kept some let - ters by his
4. I went to see him just to -

Verse 3:
He kept some letters by his bed, dated 1962.
He had underlined in red every single, "I love you".

Verse 4:
I went to see him just today, oh, but I didn't see no tears;
All dressed up to go away, first time I'd seen him smile in years.
(To Chorus:)

Verse 5: *(Spoken)*
You know, she came to see him one last time.
We all wondered if she would.
And it came running through my mind,
This time he's over her for good. (To Chorus:)

HEARTACHES BY THE NUMBER

Words and Music by
HARLAN HOWARD

HELP ME MAKE IT THROUGH THE NIGHT

Words and Music by
KRIS KRISTOFFERSON

HEY, GOOD LOOKIN'

Words and Music by
HANK WILLIAMS

Moderately

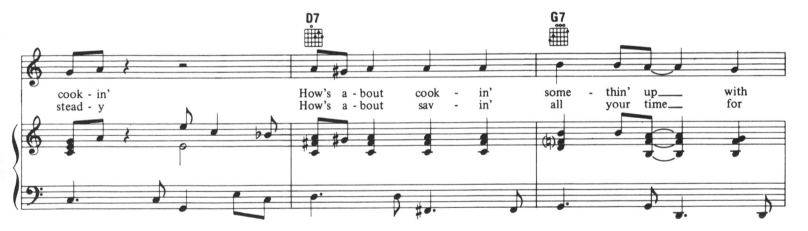

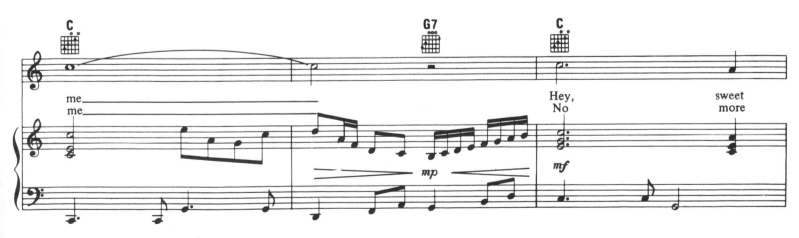

112

ba - by,
look - in', I

Don't _____ you think may - be
know _____ I've been took - en

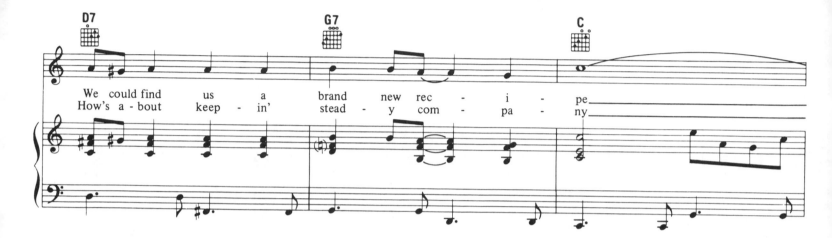

D7   **G7**   **C**

We could find us a brand new rec - i - pe _____
How's a - bout us keep - in' stead - y com - pa - ny _____

C7   **F**   **C**

I got a hot rod Ford and a two dol - lar bill and
I'm gon - na throw my date book o - ver the fence and

F   **C**   **F**

I know a spot right o - ver the hill ___ There's so - da pop and the
find me ___ one right for five or ten cents ___ I'll keep it 'til it's ___

danc-in's free, so if you wan-na have fun come a-long with me___
cov-ered with age___ 'Cause I'm writ-in' your name down on ev-'ry page___

Hey, Good Look-in' What-cha got cook-in'
Hey, Good Look-in' What-cha got cook-in'

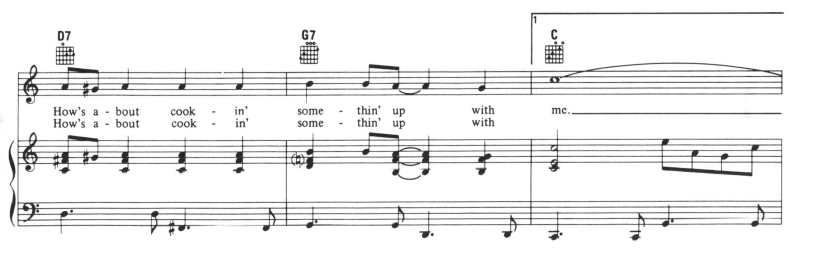

How's a-bout cook-in' some-thin' up with me.___
How's a-bout cook-in' some-thin' up with

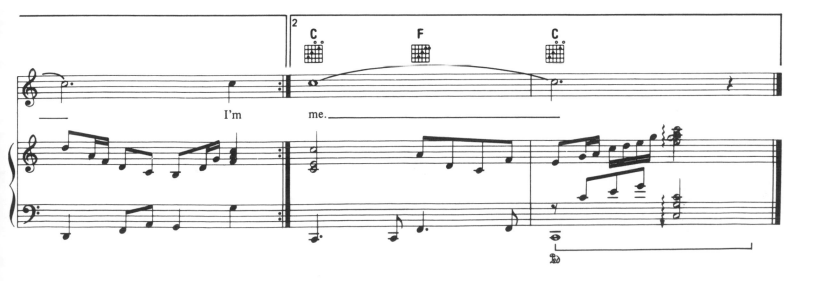

I'm me.___

(Hey, Won't You Play)
ANOTHER SOMEBODY DONE SOMEBODY WRONG SONG

Words and Music by LARRY BUTLER
and CHIPS MOMAN

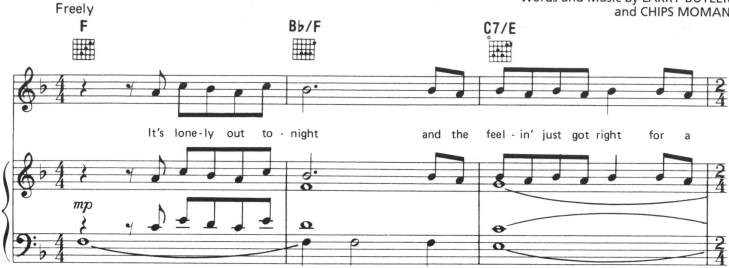

It's lone-ly out to-night and the feel-in' just got right for a

brand new love ___ song, Some-bod-y done some-bod-y

wrong song. Hey won't you play an-oth-er

I CAN'T HELP IT
(If I'm Still in Love with You)

Words and Music by
HANK WILLIAMS

Mournfully

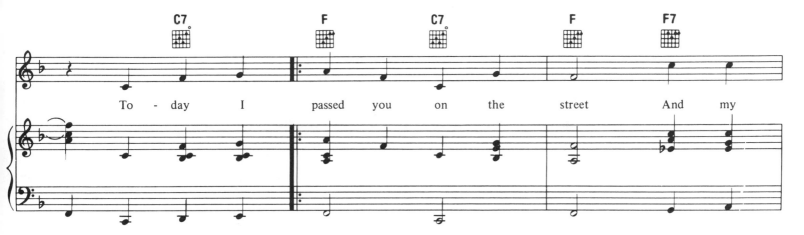

To-day I passed you on the street And my

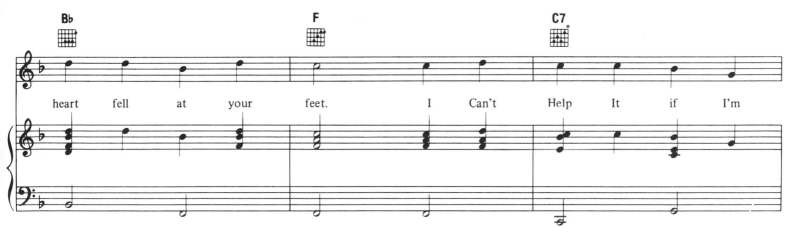

heart fell at your feet. I Can't Help It if I'm

still in love with you._____ Some - bod - y

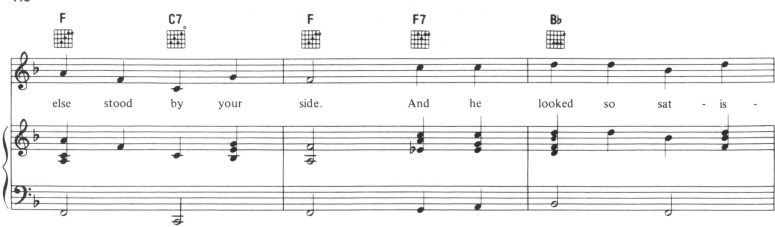

else stood by your side. And he looked so sat - is -

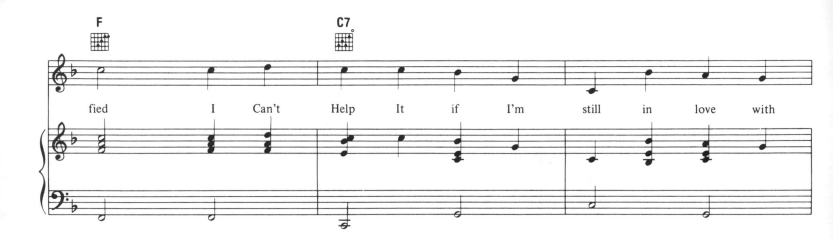

fied I Can't Help It if I'm still in love with

you. _____ { A pic - ture from the
{ It's hard to know an -

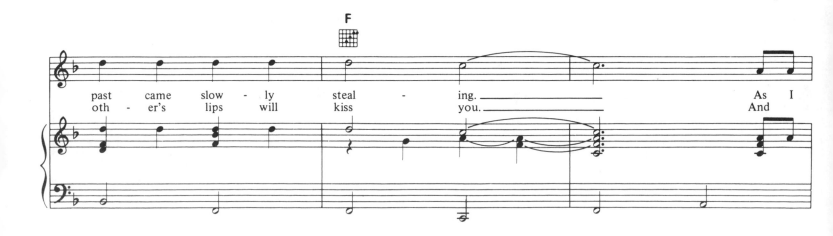

past came slow - ly steal - ing. _____ As I
oth - er's lips will kiss you. _____ And

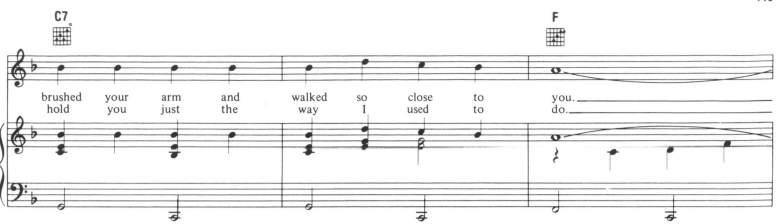

brushed your arm and the walked so close to you._____
hold you just and the way I used to do._____

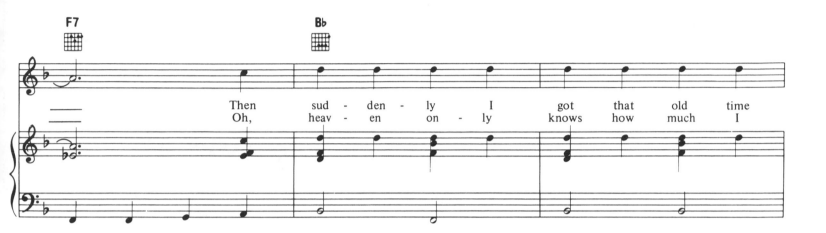

_____ Then sud - den - ly I got that old time
Oh, heav - en on - ly knows how much I

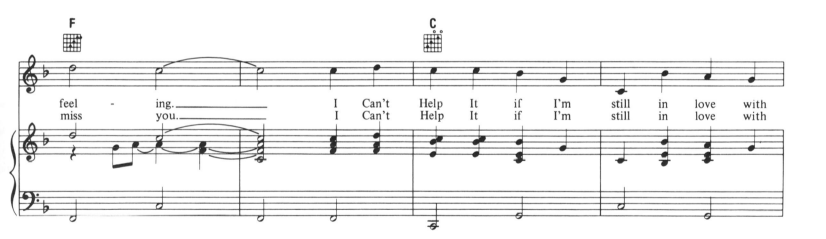

feel - ing._____ I Can't Help It if I'm still in love with
miss you._____ I Can't Help It if I'm still in love with

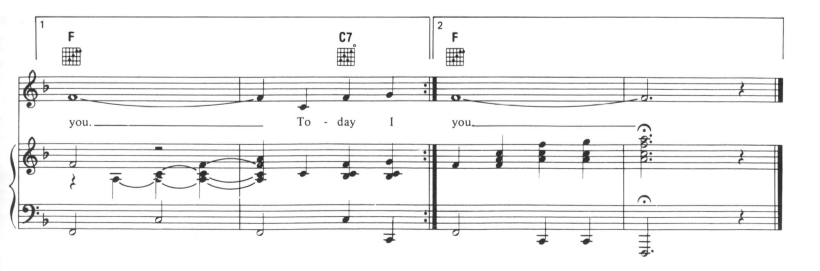

you._____ To - day I you._____

I CAN'T STOP LOVING YOU

Words and Music by
DON GIBSON

I FALL TO PIECES

Words and Music by HANK COCHRAN
and HARLAN HOWARD

An Easy "Two"

I
I

fall _____ to piec - es _____
fall _____ to piec - es _____

___ each time I see you a - gain. _____
___ each time some - one speaks your name. _____

___ I
___ I

fall _____ to piec - es. _____
fall _____ to piec - es. _____

I JUST FALL IN LOVE AGAIN

Words and Music by LARRY HERBSTRITT, STEPHEN H. DORFF,
GLORIA SKLEROV and HARRY LLOYD

Slowly

Dream-in', I must be dream-in'; or am I real-ly ly-in' here with you?
Ma-gic, it must be ma-gic; the way I hold you and the night just seems to fly.

Ba-by, you take me in your arms and though I'm wide a-wake I know my dream is com-in' true.
Eas-y for you to take me to a star, heav-en is that mo-ment when I look in-to your eyes.

And oh, I Just

I LOVED 'EM EVERY ONE

Words and Music by
PHIL SAMPSON

for their charms,___ hold-ing me in their arms,___ and I

hope they had some fun.

fun.

Repeat and Fade

I SAW THE LIGHT

Words and Music by
HANK WILLIAMS

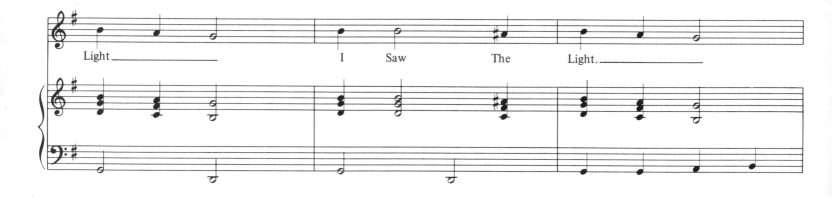

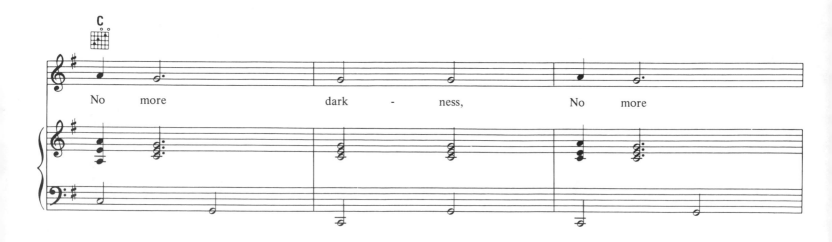

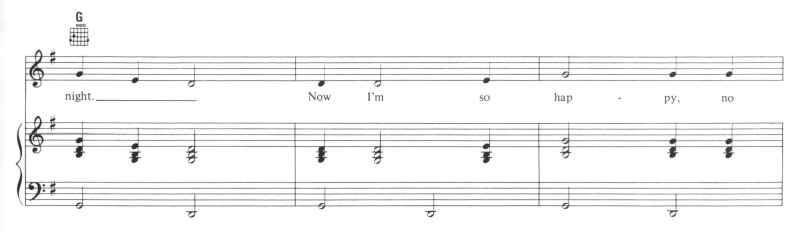

night._____ Now I'm so hap - py, no

sor - row in sight._____ Praise The

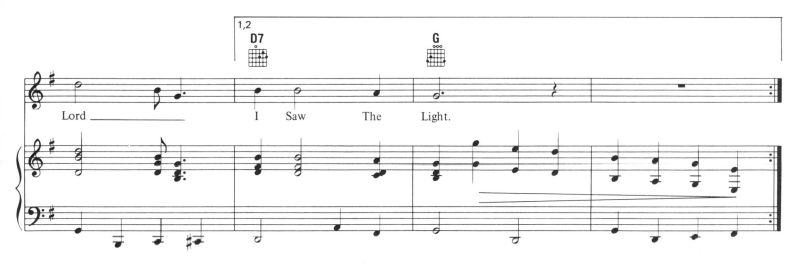

Lord _____ I Saw The Light.

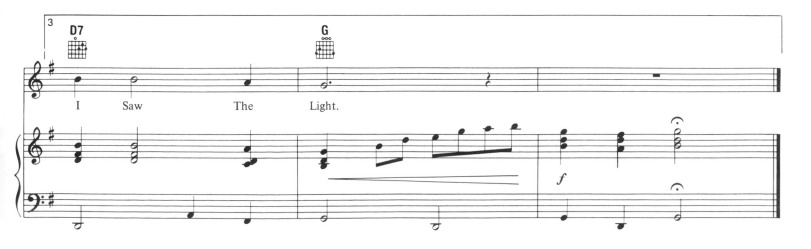

I Saw The Light.

IF TOMORROW NEVER COMES

Words and Music by KENT BLAZY
and GARTH BROOKS

Some-times late at night, ___
See additional lyrics

I lie a-wake and watch _ her sleep - ing. ___

She's lost in peace - ful dreams, _ so I turn

Additional Lyrics

2. 'Cause I've lost loved ones in my life.
   Who never knew how much I loved them.
   Now I live with the regret
   That my true feelings for them never were revealed.
   So I made a promise to myself
   To say each day how much she means to me
   And avoid that circumstance
   Where there's no second chance to tell her how I feel. ('Cause)
   Chorus

IT WAS ALMOST LIKE A SONG

Lyric by HAL DAVID
Music by ARCHIE JORDAN

JAMBALAYA
(On the Bayou)

Words and Music by
HANK WILLIAMS

Moderately

Good-bye, Joe, me got-ta go,___ me oh
daux, Fon-tain-eaux, the me place is

my oh___ Me got-ta go pole the
buzz-in'___ Kin-folk come to see Y-

pi-rogue down the bay-ou___ My Y-
vonne___ by the doz-en___ Dress in

vonne,   the sweet - est   one,   me oh my oh _____ Son of a
style   and go hog   wild,   me oh my oh _____ Son of a

gun,   we'll have   big   fun   on   the   bay - ou _____
gun,   we'll have   big   fun   on   the   bay - ou _____

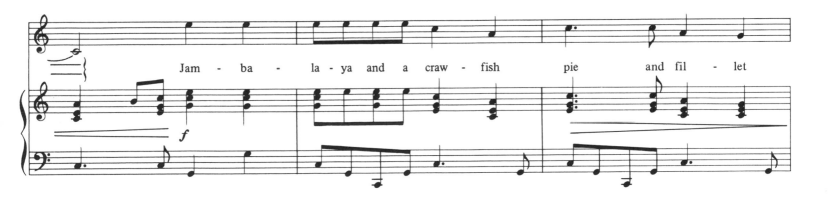

Jam - ba - la - ya and a craw - fish pie and fil - let

gum - bo _____ 'Cause to - night I'm gon - na

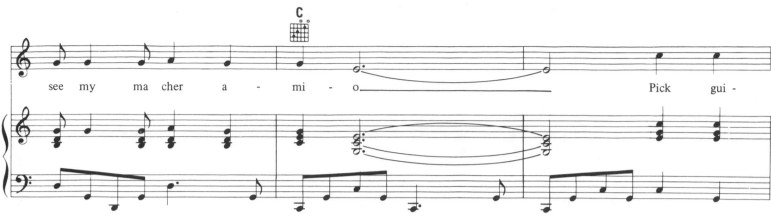

see my ma cher a - mi - o_____ Pick gui-

tar, fill fruit jar and be gay - o_____ Son of a

gun, we'll have big fun on the bay - ou_____

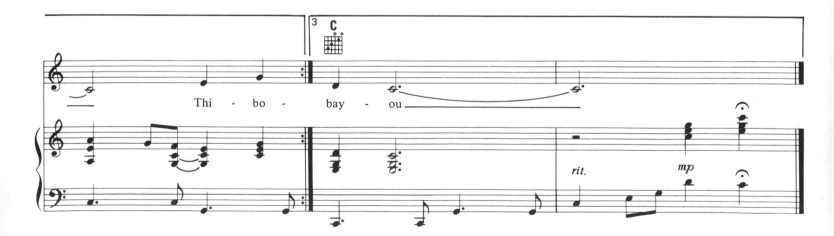

Thi - bo - bay - ou_____

3. Settle down far from town, get me a pirogue
And I'll catch all the fish in the bayou
Swap my mon to buy Yvonne what whe need-o
Son of a gun, we'll have big fun on the bayou

THE KEEPER OF THE STARS

Words and Music by KAREN STALEY,
DANNY MAYO and DICKEY LEE

It was __ no ac - ci - dent, __
Soft moon - light on your face, __

me find - ing you.
oh, how __ you shine.

Some - one __ had a hand in it __
It takes __ my __ breath a - way __

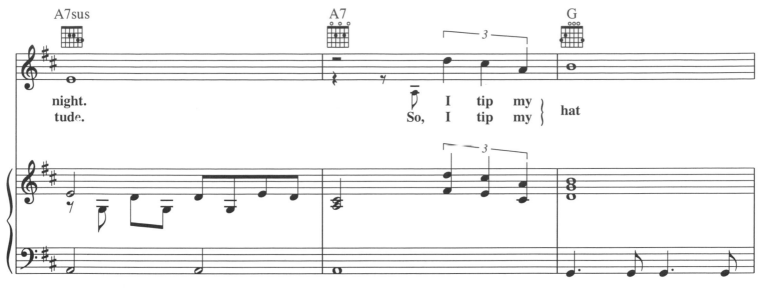

night.
tude.
So, I tip my hat

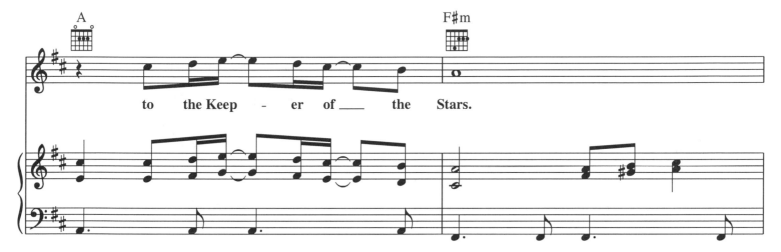

to the Keep - er of ___ the Stars.

He sure knew what he ___ was do - in' ___

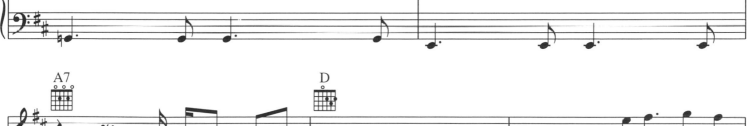

when he joined these two hearts.
I hold ev - 'ry -

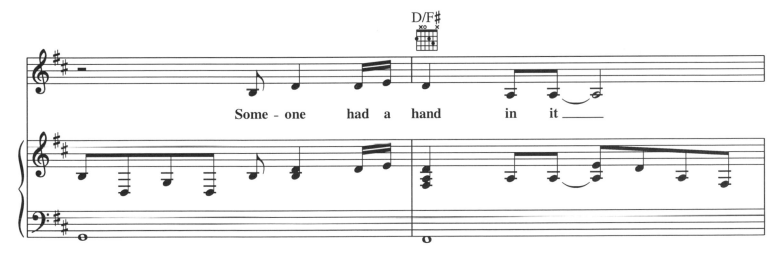
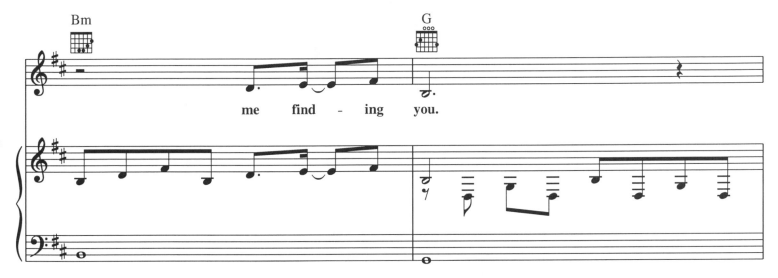

KING OF THE ROAD

Words and Music by
ROGER MILLER

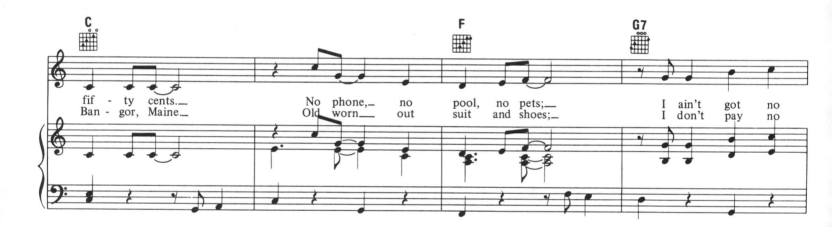

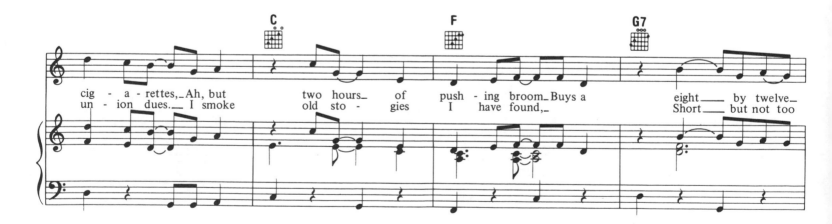

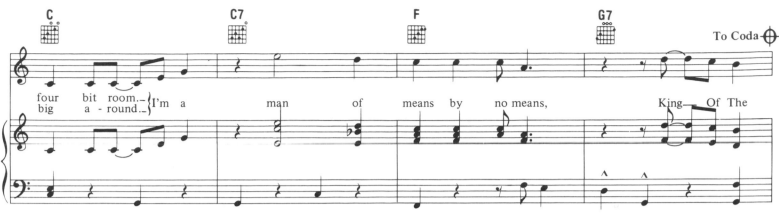

four bit room.— I'm a   man   of   means   by   no means,   King— Of The
big   a - round.—{

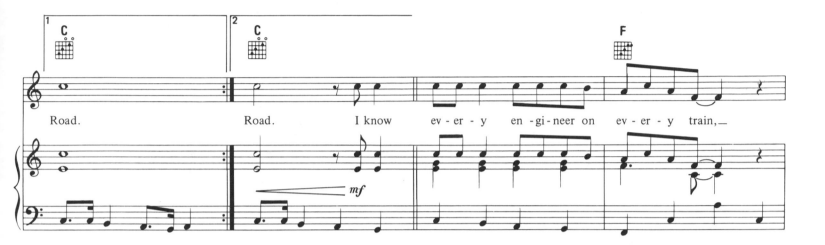

Road.   Road.   I know   ev - er - y   en - gi - neer on   ev - er - y   train,—

All   of   the   chil - dren   and   all   of   their   names—   And   ev - er - y   hand - out   in   ev - er - y   town,—   And

ev - 'ry lock that ain't locked when   no one's a - round.   I sing

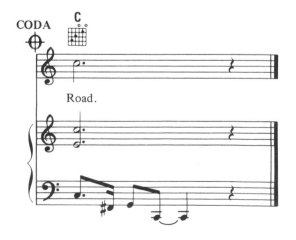

Road.

LAST DATE

By FLOYD CRAMER

Slowly

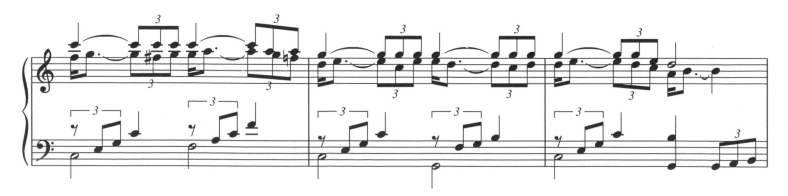

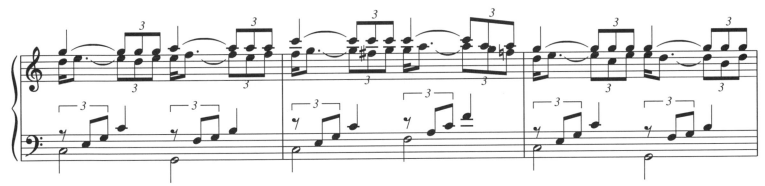

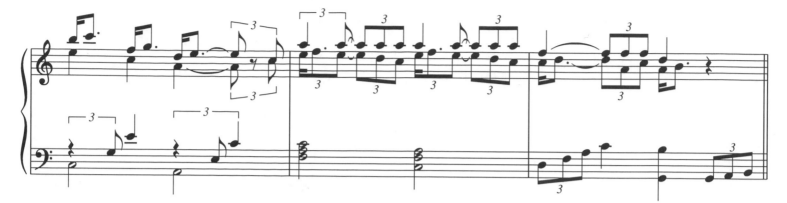

LOST IN THE FIFTIES TONIGHT
(In the Still of the Nite)

Words and Music by MIKE REID,
TROY SEALS and FRED PARRIS

1. Close your eyes ba - by,___ fol - low my heart,___
2. *See additional lyrics*

call on the mem - 'ries___ here in the dark.___ We'll let the mag - ic___

take us a - way,___ back to the feel - ing we

shared when__ they'd__ play: In the still of the nite, ___ hold__ me

dar - ling___ hold__ me tight._____ Oh,_____ shoo - doop, shoo - be doo,

shoo - doop, doo; so___ real, so___ right, lost in the Fif - ties to -

night.

Repeat ad lib. and Fade

night. Shoo-doop, shoo-be doo,

shoo-doop, shoo-be doo, shoo-doop, shoo-be doo, shoo-doop, shoo-be doo.

Additional Lyrics

These precious hours, we know can't survive.
Love's all that matters while the past is alive.
Now and for always, till time disappears,
We'll hold each other whenever we hear:

LOVE WITHOUT END, AMEN

Words and Music by
AARON G. BARKER

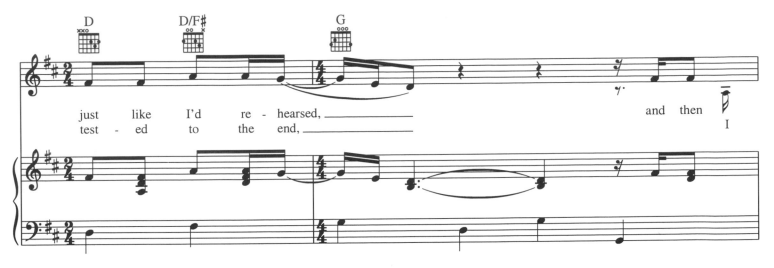

just like I'd re-hearsed, _____ and then I
test - ed to the end, _____

stood there on those trem-blin' knees_ and wait - ed for __ the worst.__
took my Dad-dy's se - cret and I passed it on __ to him. __

And he said,
I said,
"Let me tell __ you a se - cret_ a -

bout a fa - ther's_ love, a se - cret that_ my_____ Dad-dy said_ was

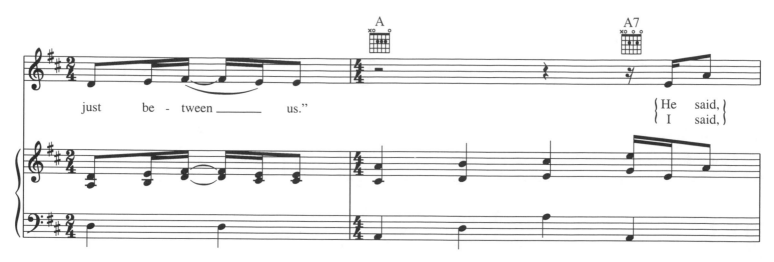

just be - tween _____ us."

{ He said, }
{ I said, }

"Dad - dys don't _ just love _ their chil - dren ev - 'ry now _ and then,

_____ it's a love with - out end, _____ A - men."

It's a love with - out end, _____ A - men.

When ... Last

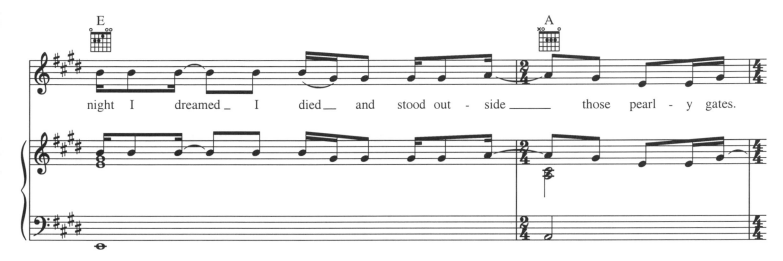

night I dreamed __ I died __ and stood out - side _____ those pearl - y gates.

When sud-den - ly, __ I re - al - ized __ there must be some __ mis-take.

If they know half the things ___ I've done they'll __

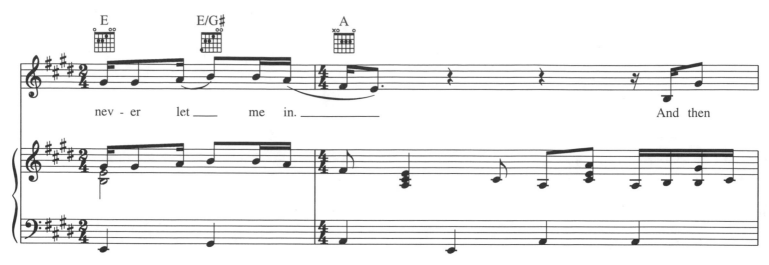

nev - er let ___ me in. _____ And then

some - where from the oth - er side I heard these words a - gain. ___

___ And they said, Let me tell ___ you a se - cret ___ a -

bout _ a fa - ther's _ love, a se - cret that _ my ___ dad - dy said ___ was

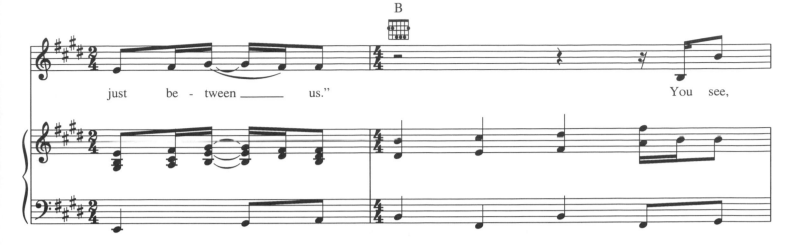

just be - tween _____ us." You see,

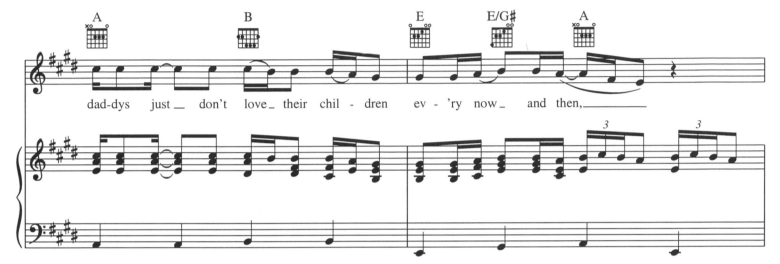

dad-dys just _ don't love _ their chil - dren ev - 'ry now _ and then, _____

it's a love with-out end, _ A - men. It's a

love with-out end, _ A - men.

LUCKENBACH, TEXAS
(Back to the Basics of Love)

Words and Music by BOBBY EMMONS
and CHIPS MOMAN

The on-ly two things in life that make it worth liv-in' is

gui-tars that tune good and firm feel-in' wo-men. I don't need my name in the mar-quee

lights; I got my song and I got you with me to-night. May-be it's time we got

MAKE THE WORLD GO AWAY

Words and Music by
HANK COCHRAN

Moderately slow

Do you re-mem-ber when you loved me
hurt you,

be - fore the world took me a-
I'll make it up___ day by

stray?
day.

If you do then for - give me,
Just say you love me like you used to

And make the world___ go a - way.
And make the world___ go a - way.

MAMMAS DON'T LET YOUR BABIES GROW UP TO BE COWBOYS

Words and Music by ED BRUCE
and PATSY BRUCE

Country Waltz

Mam - mas don't let your ba - bies grow up __ to be cow - boys.

Don't let 'em pick gui - tars and

drive them old trucks. Make 'em be doc - tors and law - yers and

173

MY ELUSIVE DREAMS

Words and Music by CURLY PUTMAN
and BILLY SHERRILL

1. You fol-lowed me ___ to Tex-as, You fol-lowed me _ to U-tah,
2,3 *(See additional lyrics)*

We did-n't find it there so we moved on. ___ You

fol-lowed me ___ to Al-a-bam', Things looked good in Bir-ming-ham,

2. You had my child in Memphis, I heard of work in Nashville,
   We didn't find it there so we moved on.
   To a small farm in Nebraska to a gold mine in Alaska,
   We didn't find it there so we moved on. (Chorus)

3. And now we've left Alaska because there was no gold mine,
   But this time only two of us move on.
   Now all we have is each other and a little memory to cling to,
   And still you won't let me go on alone. (Chorus)

PUT YOUR HAND IN THE HAND

Words and Music by
GENE MacLELLAN

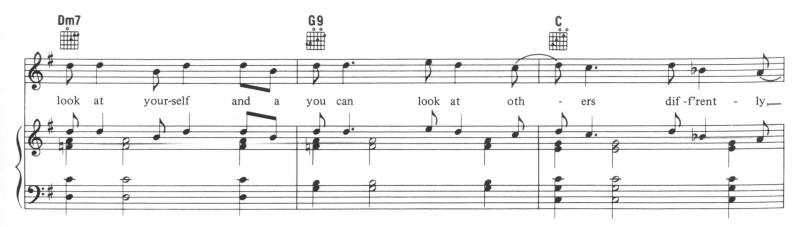

look at your-self and a you can look at oth - ers dif -f'rent - ly,___

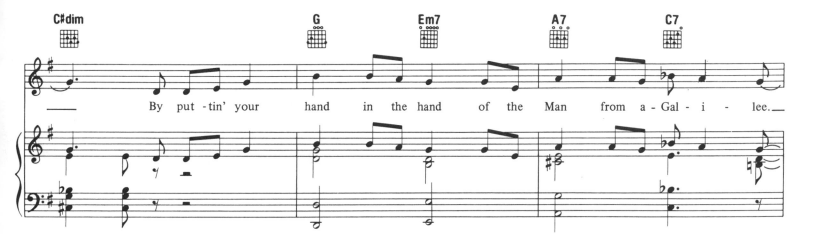

___ By put -tin' your hand in the hand of the Man from a - Gal - i - lee.___

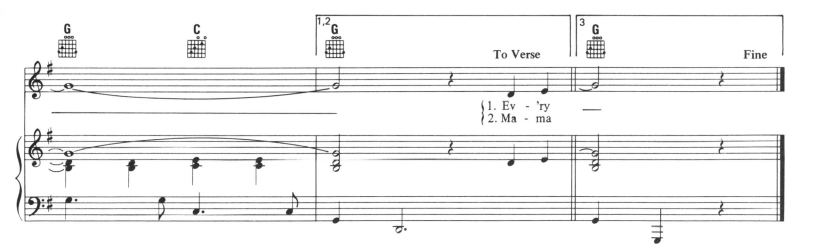

To Verse Fine

1. Ev - 'ry ___
2. Ma - ma

Verse

time I look___ in -to the Ho - ly Book___ I wan -na trem -ble,_____
taught me how to pray be -fore I reached the age_____ of sev - en,_____

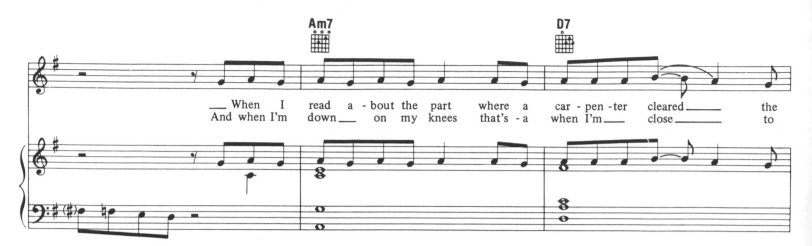

When I read a-bout the part where a car-pen-ter cleared_____ the
And when I'm down_____ on my knees that's-a when I'm_____ close_____ to

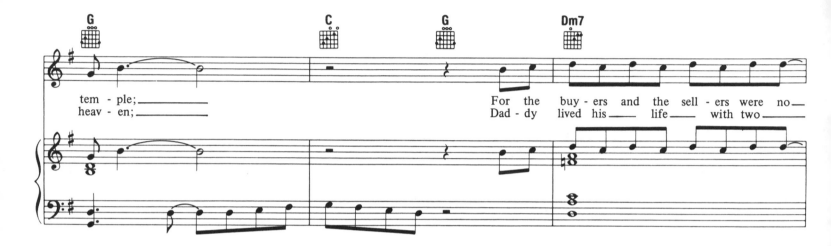

tem - ple;_____
heav - en;_____

For the buy - ers and the sell - ers were no_____
Dad - dy lived his_____ life_____ with two_____

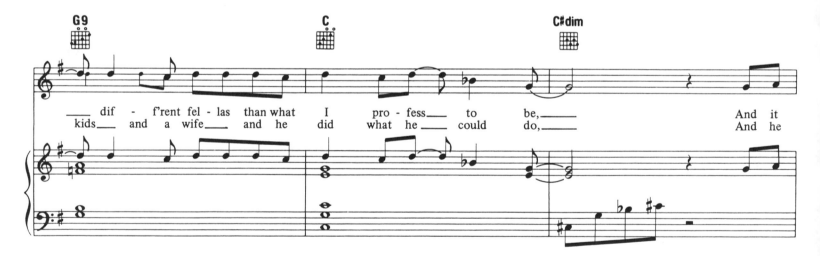

_____ dif - f'rent fel - las than what I pro - fess_____ to be,_____ And it
kids_____ and a wife_____ and he did what he_____ could do,_____ And he

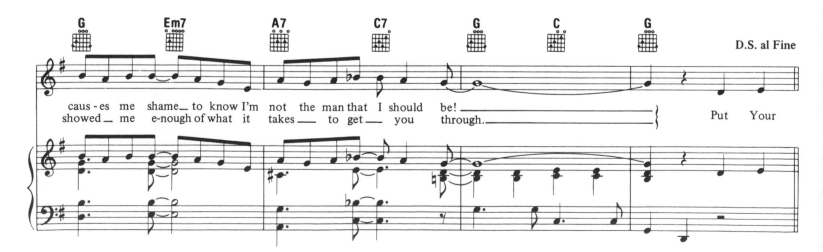

D.S. al Fine

caus - es me shame_____ to know I'm not the man that I should be!
showed_____ me e-nough of what it takes_____ to get_____ you through._____

Put Your

RHINESTONE COWBOY

Words and Music by
LARRY WEISS

Cow - boy riding out on a horse in a star spang - led ro - de - o.

Rhine - stone Cow - boy, get - tin'

cards and let - ters from peo - ple I don't ev - en know;___ of - fers com - ing o - ver the

phone.

(D.C.) D.S. and Fade

RELEASE ME

Words and Music by ROBERT YOUNT,
EDDIE MILLER and DUB WILLIAMS

Moderately slow

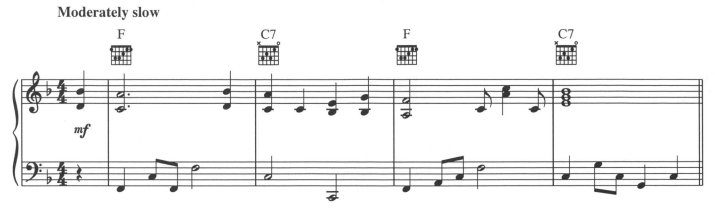

Please ___ re - lease me, let me go, ___
I ___ have found a new love, dear, ___
Please ___ re - lease me, can't you see ___

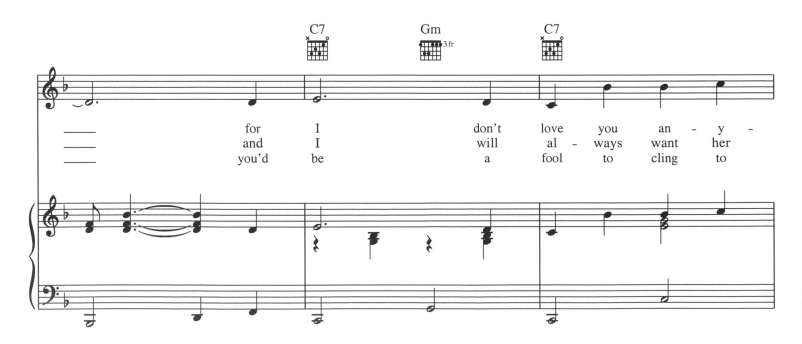

___ for I ___ don't love you an - y -
___ and I ___ will al - ways want her
___ you'd be ___ a fool to cling to

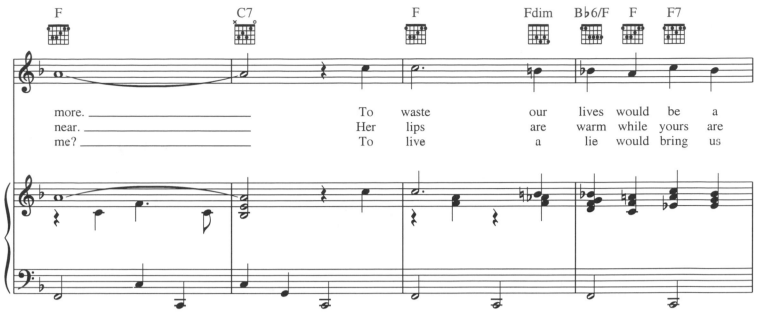

more. _____
near. _____
me? _____

To waste   our   lives would be a
Her lips   are   warm while yours are
To live   a   lie would bring us

sin; _____
cold; _____
pain, _____

re - lease me   and let me love a -
re - lease me,   my dar - ling, let me
so re - lease me   and let me love a -

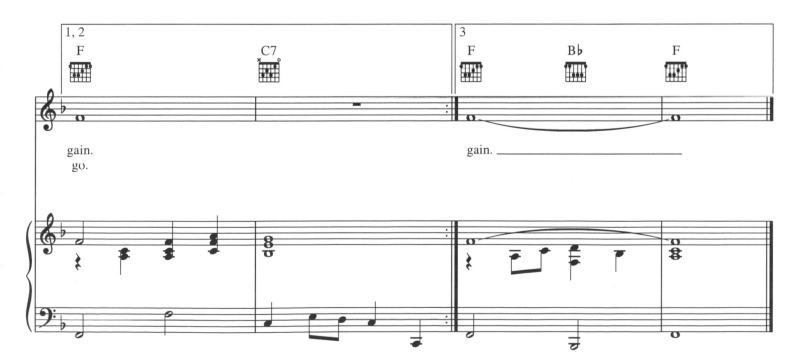

1, 2

gain.
go.

3

gain. _____

RING OF FIRE

Words and Music by MERLE KILGORE
and JUNE CARTER

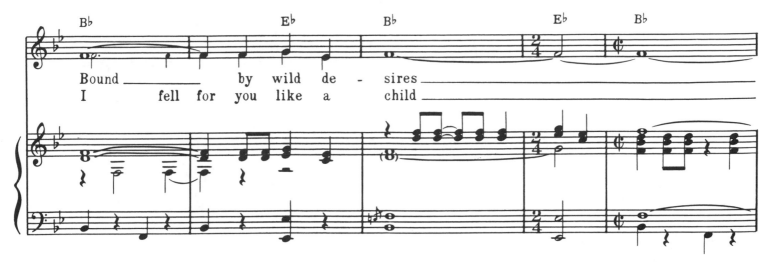

ROCKY TOP

Words and Music by BOUDLEAUX BRYANT
and FELICE BRYANT

Lively

Wish that I was on ol' Rock - y Top,
Once that two stran - gers climbed ol' Rock - y Top,

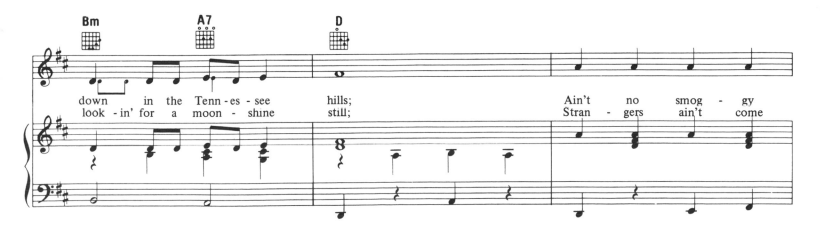

down in the Tenn - es - see hills; Ain't no smog - gy
look - in' for a moon - shine still; Stran - gers ain't come

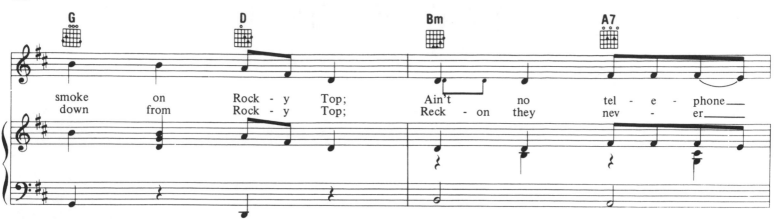

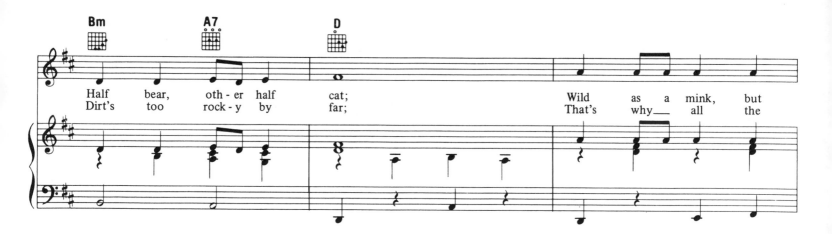

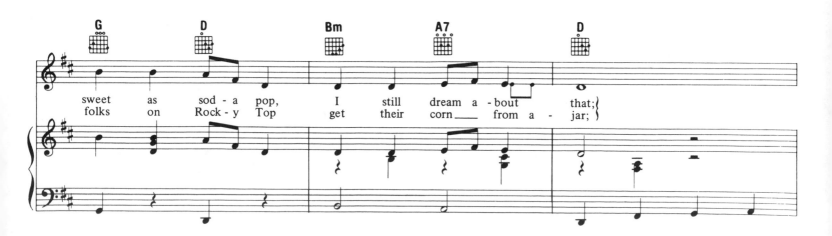

Chorus

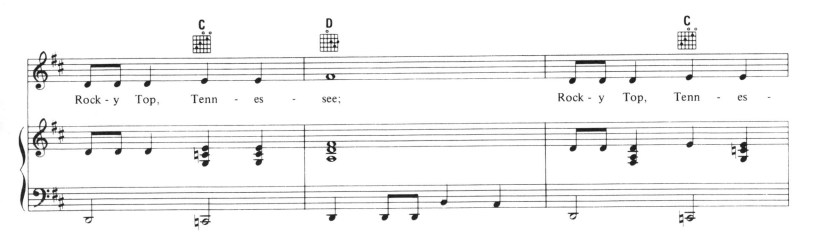

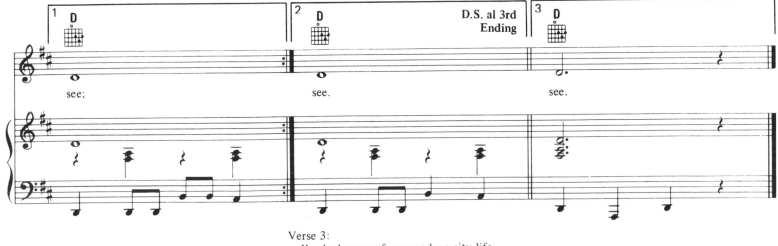

Verse 3:
I've had years of cramped-up city life
Trapped like a duck in a pen;
All I know is it's a pity life
Can't be simple again. (Chorus)

RUBY, DON'T TAKE YOUR LOVE TO TOWN

Words and Music by
MEL TILLIS

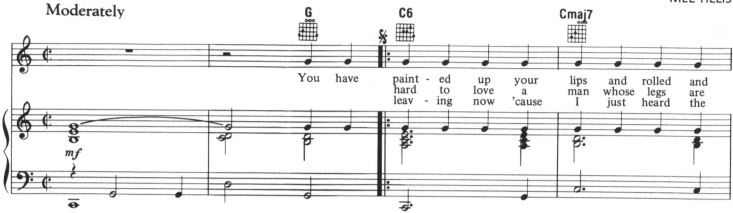

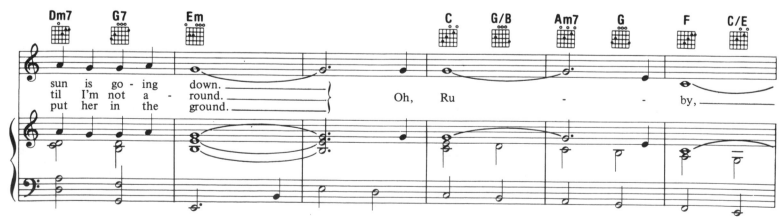

SATISFIED MIND

Words and Music by JOE "RED" HAYES
and JACK RHODES

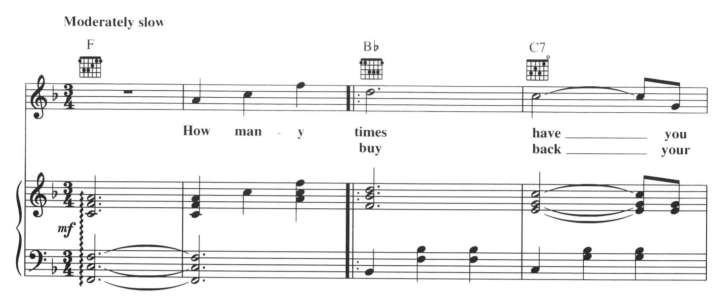

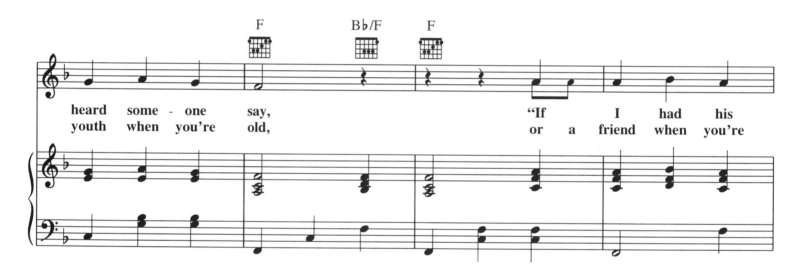

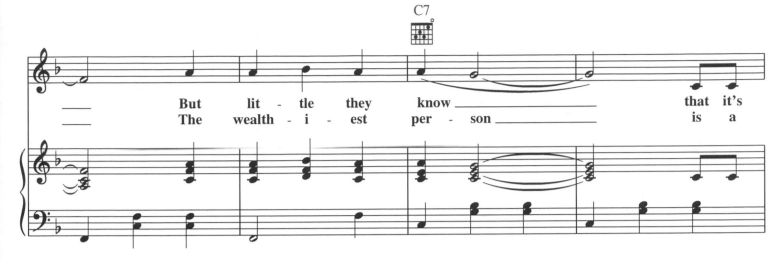

But   lit - tle   they   know _____   that   it's
The   wealth - i - est   per - son _____   is   a

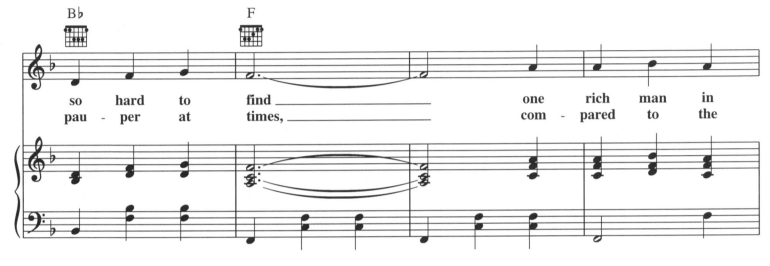

so   hard   to   find _____   one   rich   man   in
pau - per   at   times, _____   com - pared   to   the

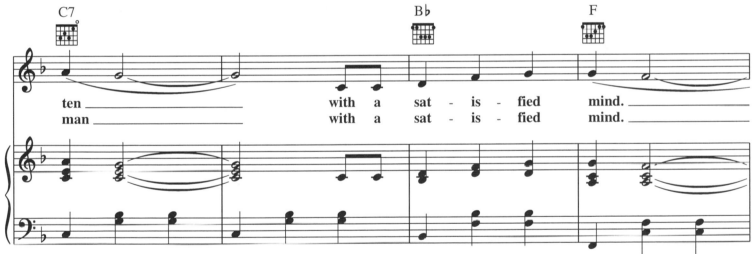

ten _____   with   a   sat - is - fied   mind. _____
man _____   with   a   sat - is - fied   mind. _____

Once   I   was   win - ning _____
When   life   has   end - ed, _____

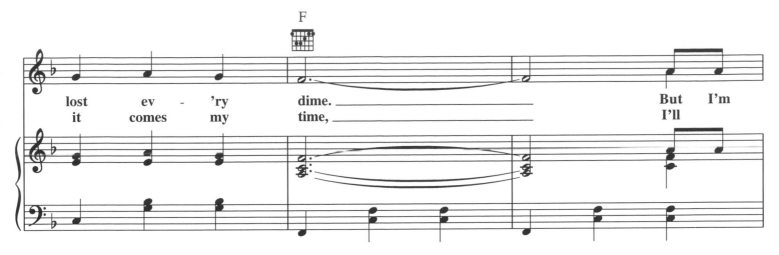

lost ev - 'ry dime. _____ But I'm
it comes my time, _____ I'll

rich - er by far _____ with a sat - is - fied
leave this old world _____

mind. _____ Mon - ey can't

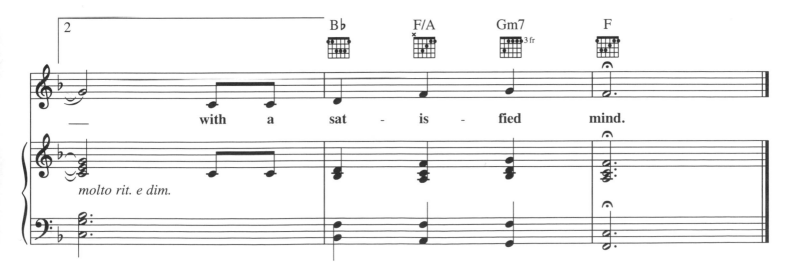

_____ with a sat - is - fied mind.

molto rit. e dim.

SIXTEEN TONS

Words and Music by
MERLE TRAVIS

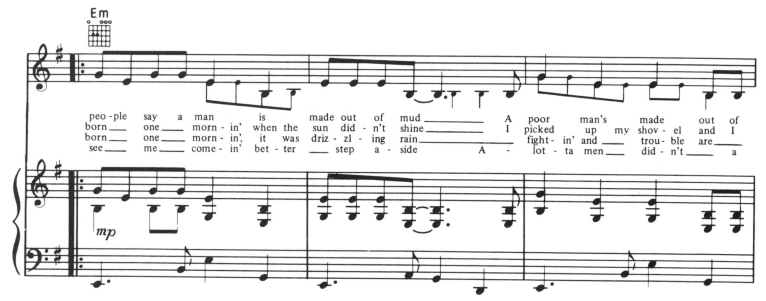

SMOKY MOUNTAIN RAIN

Words and Music by KYE FLEMING
and DENNIS MORGAN

I can't blame her for let - ting go;___ a wom - an needs some - one warm___ ___ to hold.___ I feel the rain run - ning down___ my face;___ I'll find her no mat - ter what it takes.___

D.S. and Fade

SOME DAYS ARE DIAMONDS
(Some Days Are Stone)

Words and Music by
DICK FELLER

When you ask ___ how I've been ___ here with my
Now the face ___ that I see ___ in my

out you, I'd like to say I've been fine, ___
mir-ror, more and more, is a

stran-ger and I do; ___
more and to me; more, ___ but we both ___ know the
I can

STAND BY ME

Words and Music by BEN E. KING,
JERRY LEIBER and MIKE STOLLER

Moderately, with a beat

When the

night ... has come ___
sky ... that we look up-on ___ and the land is
should tum - ble and

dark ... and the moon ___ is the on - ly light we
fall ... and the moun - tains ___ should crum - ble in - to the

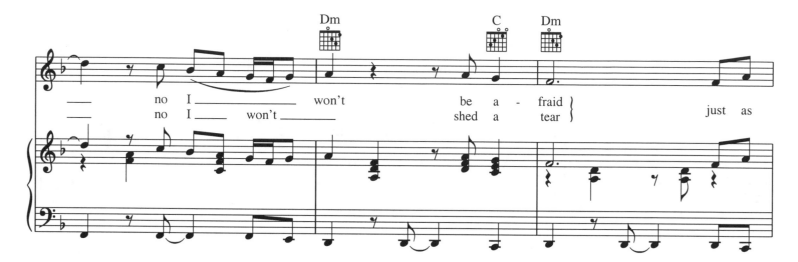

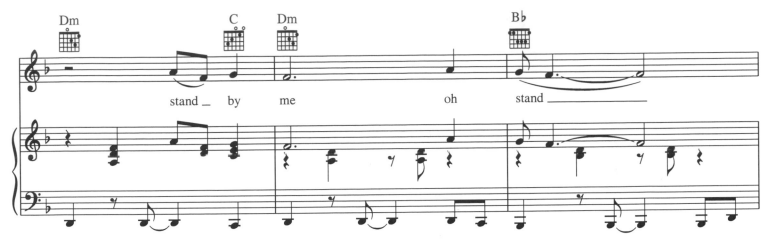

stand by me oh stand

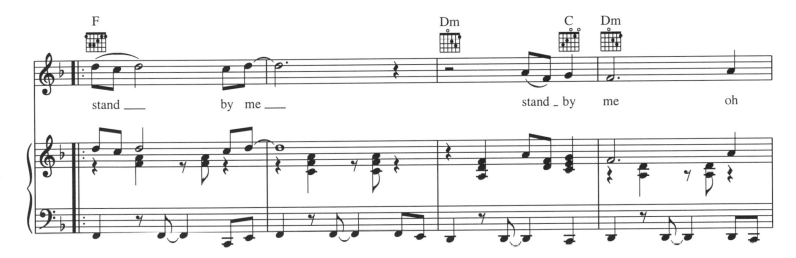

stand by me stand by me. If the Dar-ling,

stand by me stand by me oh

Repeat and Fade

stand stand by me stand by me. When-ev-er I'm in trou-ble won't you

STAND BY YOUR MAN

Words and Music by TAMMY WYNETTE
and BILLY SHERRILL

Some - times___ it's hard___ to be a wo - man,
But if___ you love him___ you'll for - give him,___

giv - ing all your love
e - ven though he's hard

to just
to un - der-

one stand.___ man.___

You'll have___
And if___ you

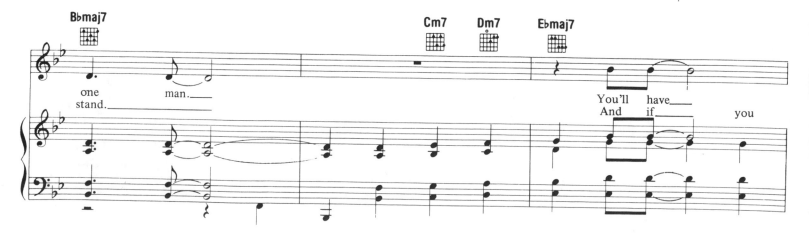

TENNESSEE WALTZ

Words and Music by REDD STEWART
and PEE WEE KING

Country Waltz

Lyrics:

I was waltz-ing with my dar-lin' to the Ten-nes - see Waltz when an old friend I hap-pened to see. In-tro-

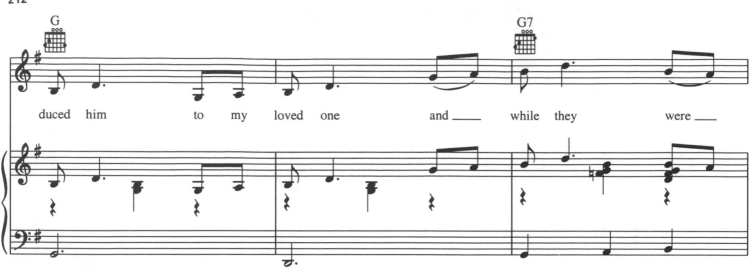

duced him to my loved one and ___ while they were ___

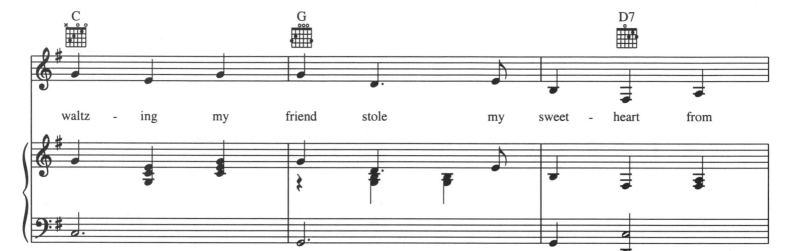

waltz - ing my friend stole my sweet - heart from

me. _____ I re - mem - ber the night and the

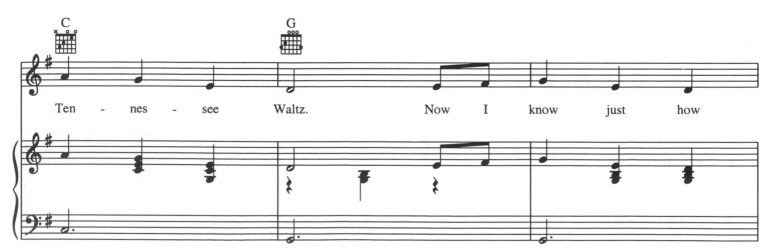

Ten - nes - see Waltz. Now I know just how

SWEET DREAMS

Words and Music by
DON GIBSON

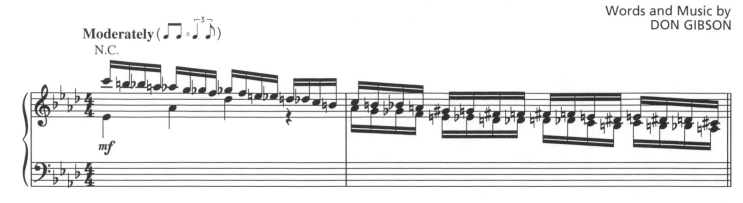

Sweet _____ dreams _ of you _____ ev - 'ry

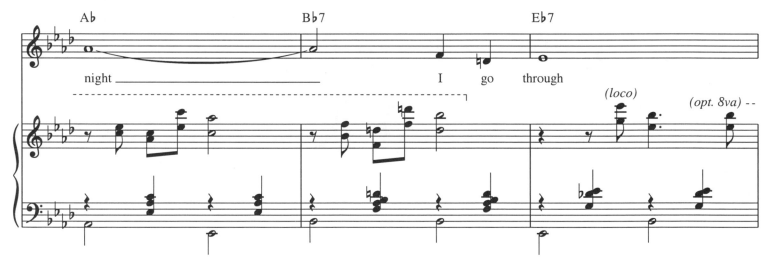

night _____ I go through

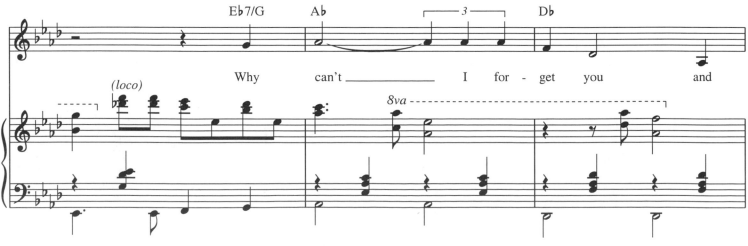

Why can't _____ I for - get you and

start my life a - new   In - stead of hav - ing

sweet dreams a - bout you.

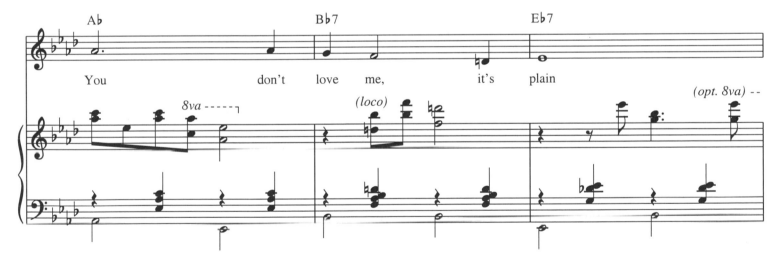

You   don't love me,   it's   plain

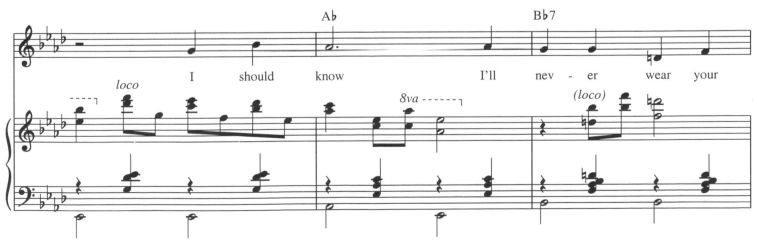

I should know   I'll nev - er wear your

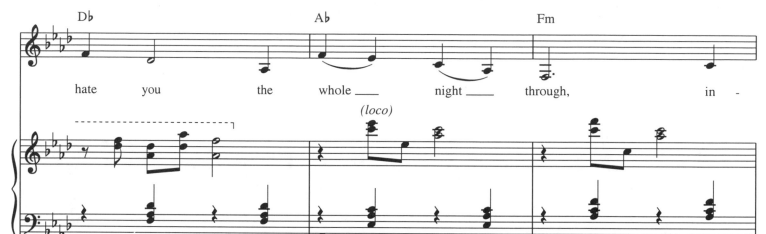

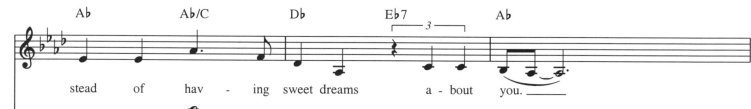

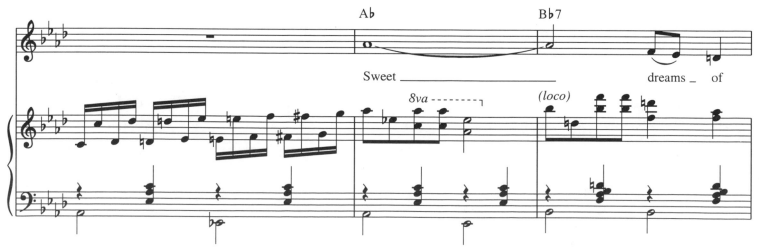

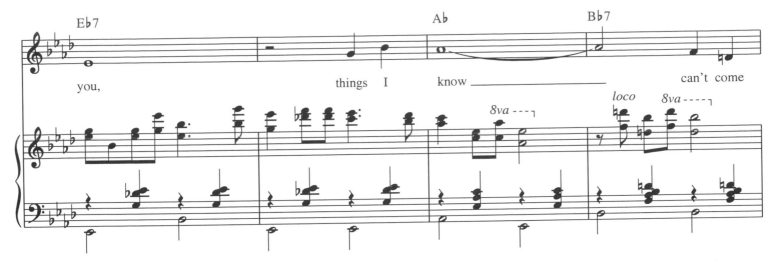

THROUGH THE YEARS

Words and Music by STEVE DORFF
and MARTY PANZER

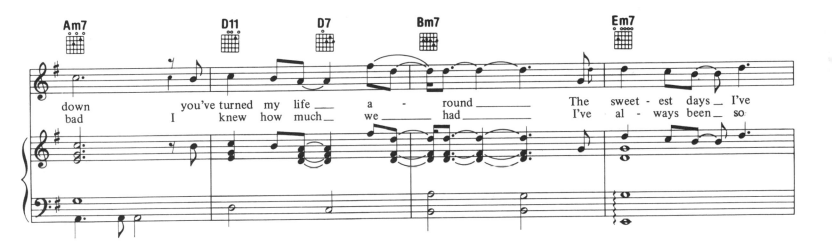

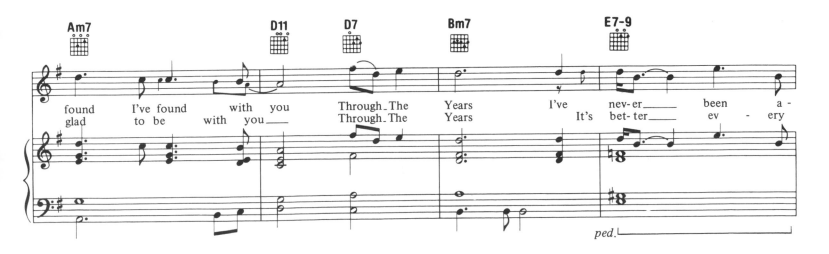

TO ALL THE GIRLS I'VE LOVED BEFORE

Lyric by HAL DAVID
Music by ALBERT HAMMOND

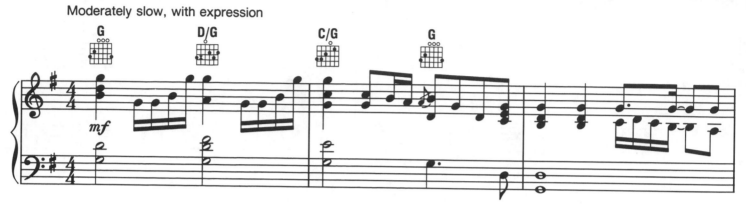

CODA

C/G   G   Eb7sus   Ab

loved be - fore.   1. To all the girls who cared for me;
                                     loved be - fore;

Bbm7

who filled my nights with ec - sta - sy;___   they live with - in my
who trav - eled in and out our door;___   we're glad they came a -

Bbm7/Eb   Eb7   Bbm7/Eb   Eb7   1 Ab   Db/Ab

heart; I'll al - ways be a part of all the girls I've loved be - fore.
long; we ded - i - cate this song to all the girls we've

To next strain 2

Ab   Db/Ab   Ab   Db/Ab   Ab

The winds of change are al - ways loved - be - fore.   2. To all the girls we've

WABASH CANNONBALL

Words and Music by
A.P. CARTER

Moderately

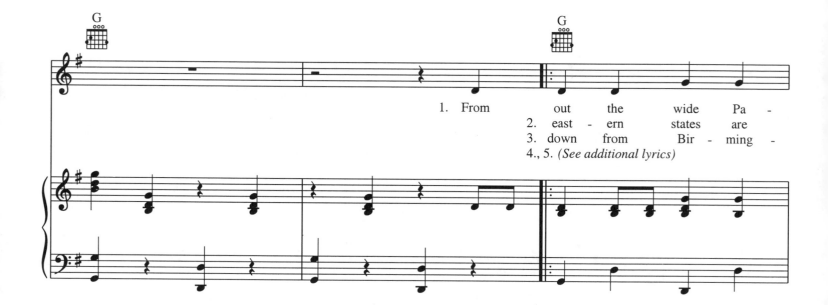

1. From out the wide Pa -
2. east - ern wide states are
3. down from Bir - ming -
4., 5. *(See additional lyrics)*

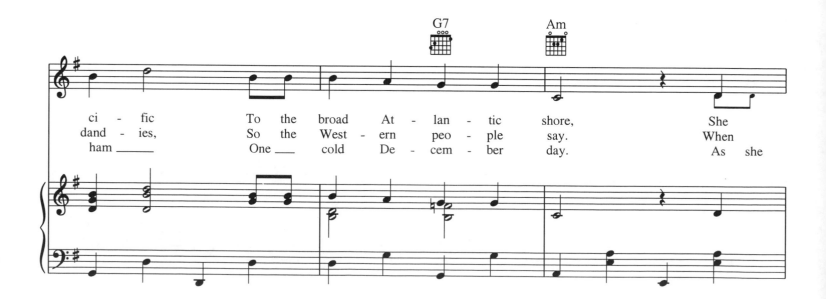

ci - fic   To the broad At - lan - tic shore,   She
dand - ies,   So the West - ern peo - ple say.   When
ham ___   One ___ cold De - cem - ber day.   As she

climbs   high _____   moun - tains   Up
she   climbed   Old   Rock   Is - land,   Took
pulled   in   to   the   sta - tion   You   could

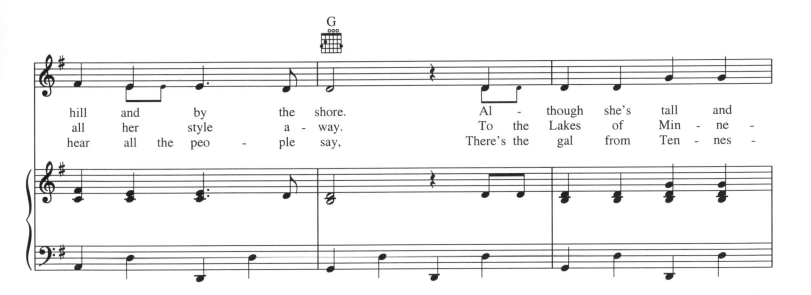

hill   and   by   the   shore.   Al - though she's   tall   and
all   her   style   a - way.   To   the   Lakes   of   Min - ne -
hear   all   the   peo - ple   say,   There's   the   gal   from   Ten - nes -

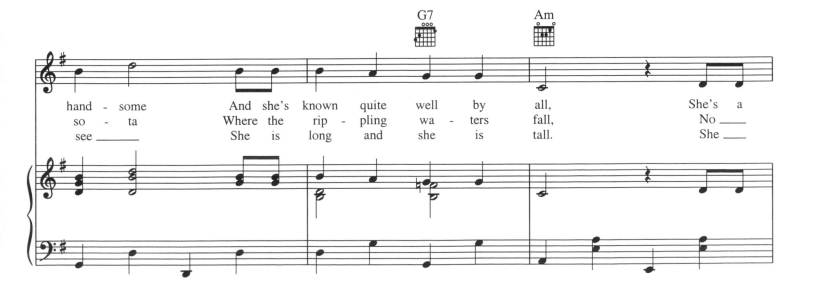

hand - some   And she's   known   quite   well   by   all,   She's   a
so - ta   Where the   rip - pling   wa - ters   fall,   No _____
see _____   She   is   long   and   she   is   tall.   She _____

reg - 'lar com - bi - na - tion of the Wa - bash Can - non -
chan - ges can be tak - en on the Wa - bash Can - non -
comes from Bir - ming - ham on the Wa - bash Can - non -

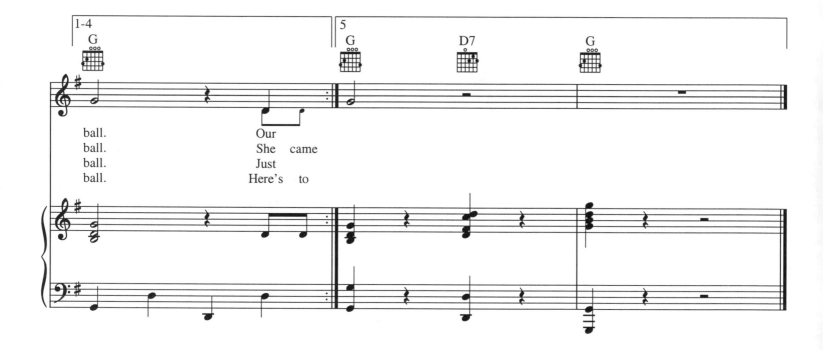

ball. Our
ball. She came
ball. Just
ball. Here's to

Additional Lyrics

4. Just listen to the jingle
   And the rumble and the roar,
   As she glides along the woodland
   To the hills and by the shore.
   Hear the mighty rush of the engine
   Hear the lonesome hoboes call,
   While she's trav'ling thru the jungle
   On the Wabash Cannonball.

5. Here's to old man daddy Claxton,
   May his name forever stand;
   May it always be remembered
   Throughout the land.
   His earthly race is over
   And the curtains 'round him fall.
   We'll carry him home to vict'ry
   On the Wabash Cannonball.

WALKING THE FLOOR OVER YOU

Words and Music by
ERNEST TUBB

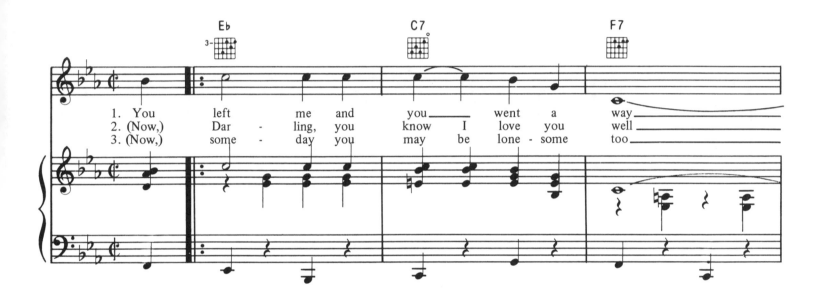

1. You   left   me   and   you____   went   a   way____
2. (Now,) Dar - ling, you   know   I   love   you   well____
3. (Now,) some - day you   may   be   lone - some too____

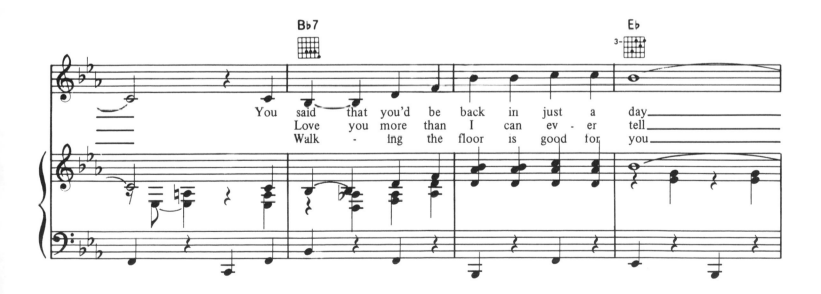

You   said   that   you'd   be   back   in   just   a   day____
Love   you   more   than   I   can   ev - er   tell____
Walk - ing   the   floor   is   good   for   you____

WALKIN' AFTER MIDNIGHT

Lyrics by DON HECHT
Music by ALAN W. BLOCK

WALKING IN THE SUNSHINE

Words and Music by
ROGER MILLER

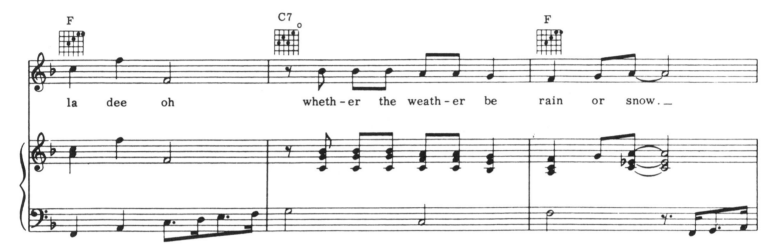

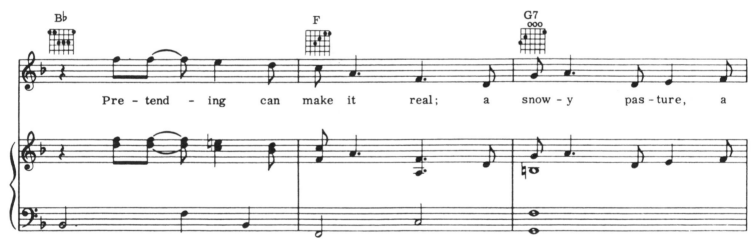

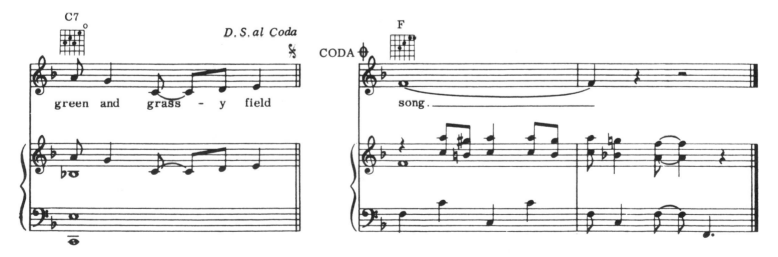

WELCOME TO MY WORLD

Words and Music by RAY WINKLER
and JOHN HATHCOCK

WHEN YOU SAY NOTHING AT ALL

Words and Music by DON SCHLITZ
and PAUL OVERSTREET

It's a-maz - ing how you can speak right to my heart.
All day long I can hear peo-ple talk - ing out loud,

With-out say - ing a word you can light up the dark.
but when you hold me near you drown out the crowd.

Try as I may I could nev - er ex - plain
Old Mis-ter Web - ster could nev - er de - fine

what I hear____ when you don't____ say a thing.____ }
what's be - ing said____ be - tween your____ heart and mine.____

The

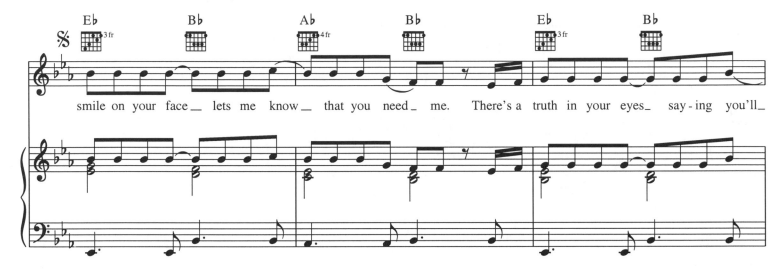

smile on your face__ lets me know__ that you need__ me. There's a truth in your eyes__ say-ing you'll__

__ nev-er leave__ me.   A touch of your hand__ says you'll catch__ me if ev - er I fall.__

Now you say it best ___   when you say noth-ing at all.___

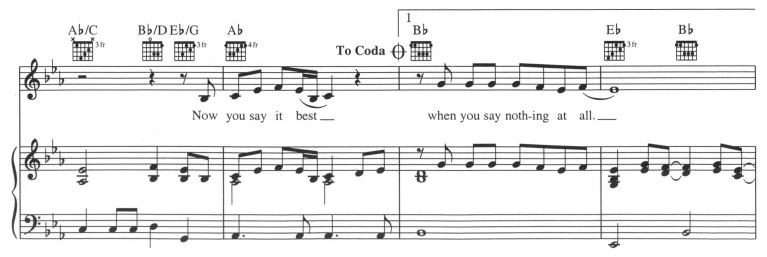

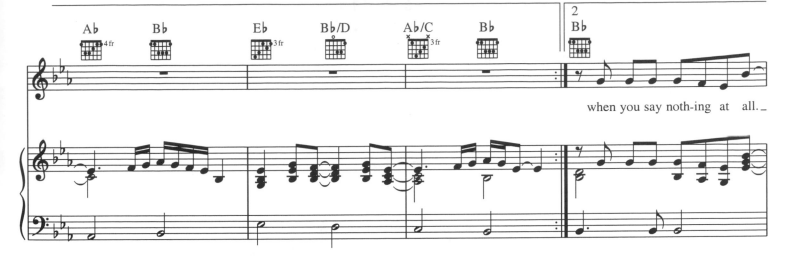

when you say noth-ing at all. _

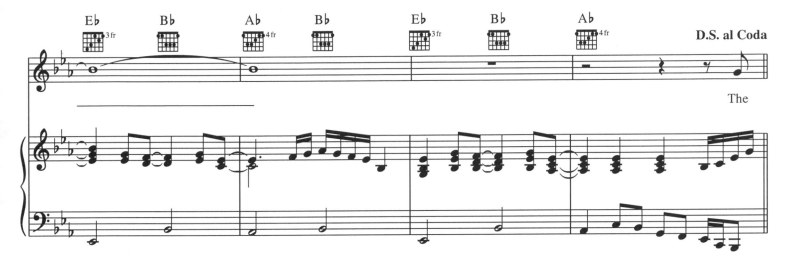

D.S. al Coda

The

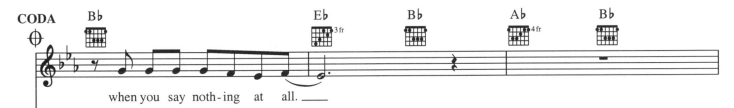

CODA

when you say noth-ing at all. _____

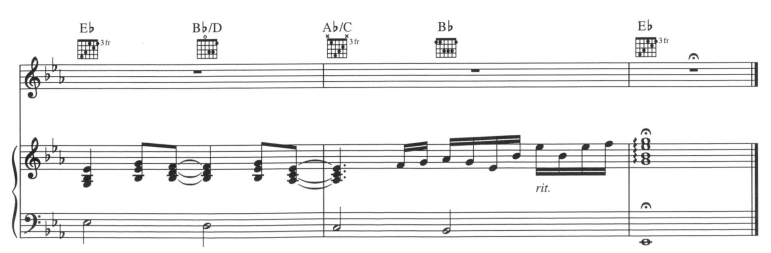

rit.

A WHITE SPORT COAT
(And a Pink Carnation)

Words and Music by
MARTY ROBBINS

Relaxed

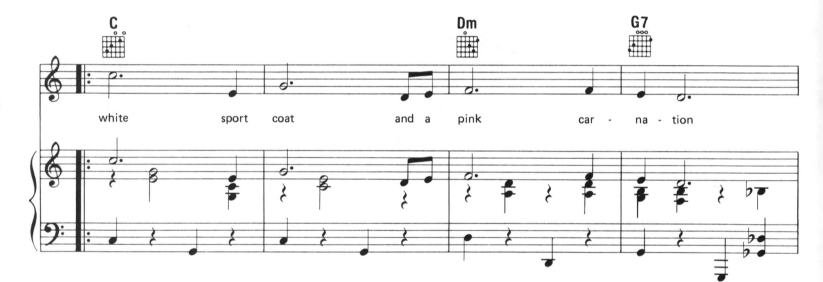

white   sport   coat   and a   pink   car - na - tion

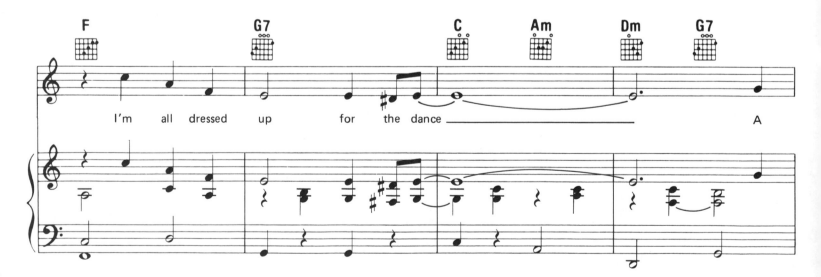

I'm   all   dressed   up   for   the   dance _____

WIDE OPEN SPACES

Words and Music by
SUSAN GIBSON

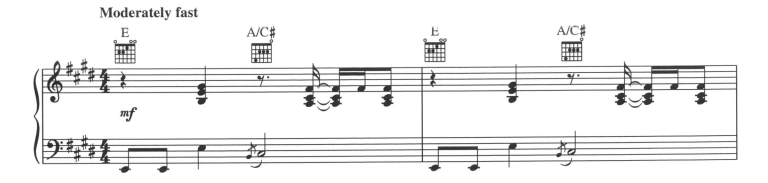

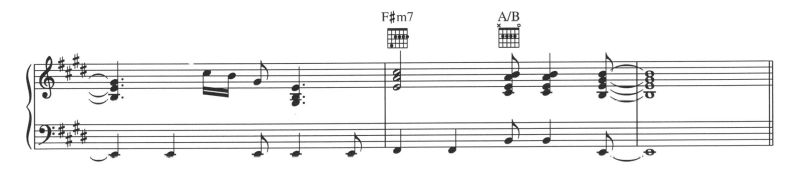

Who does-n't know what I'm talk-ing a-bout?

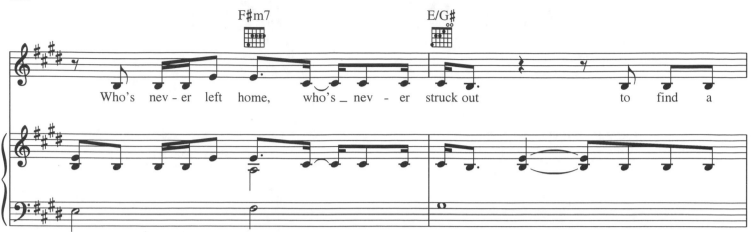

Who's nev-er left home, who's _ nev-er struck out to find a

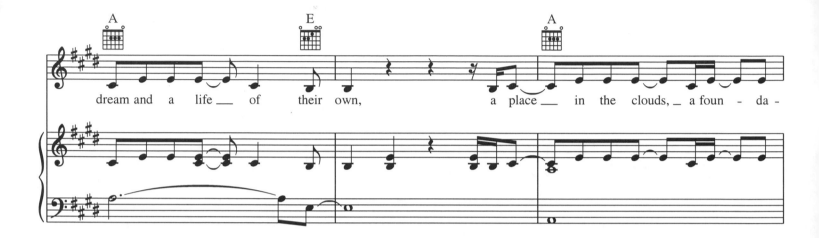

dream and a life __ of their own, a place __ in the clouds, _ a foun-da-

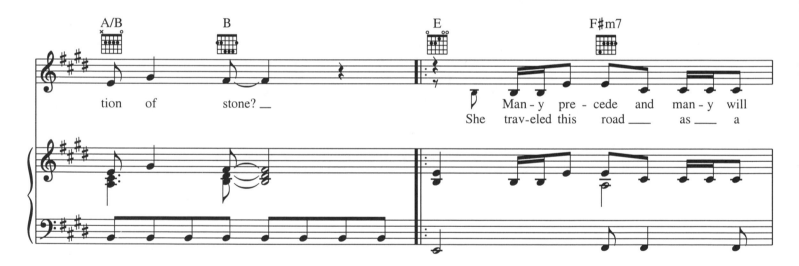

tion of stone? __

She trav-eled this road __ as __ a

Man-y pre-cede and man-y will

fol-low,
child, _

a young girl's dreams no long-er
wide-eyed and grin-ning, she nev-er

hol - low.
tired. __

It takes the shape of a place __ out __ west.
But now she won't be com - ing back with __ the

__ rest.
__ test.

But what it holds __ for her she has - n't yet __
If these are life's __ les - sons, she'll take __ this __

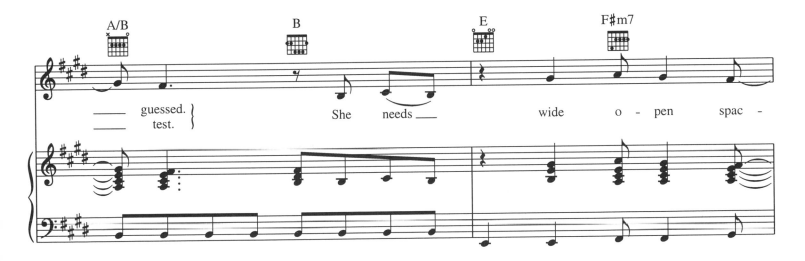

__ guessed.
__ test.

She needs __ wide o - pen spac -

- es,

room to make __ her big __ mis -

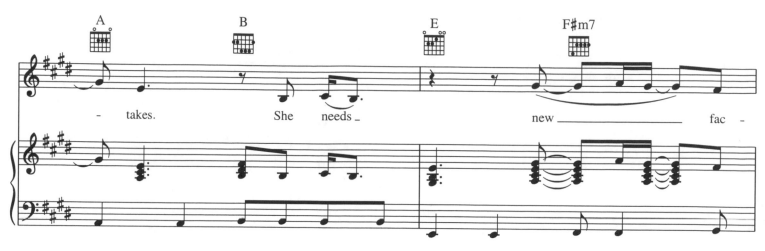

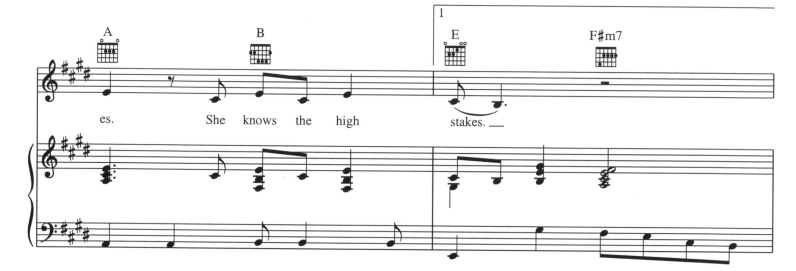

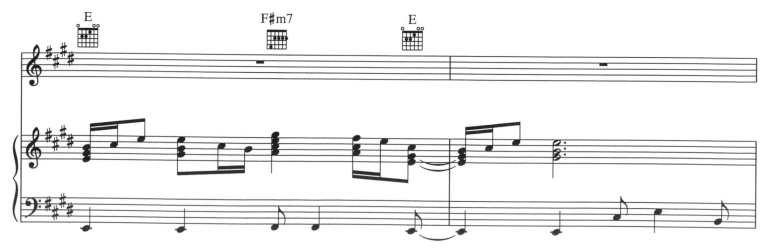

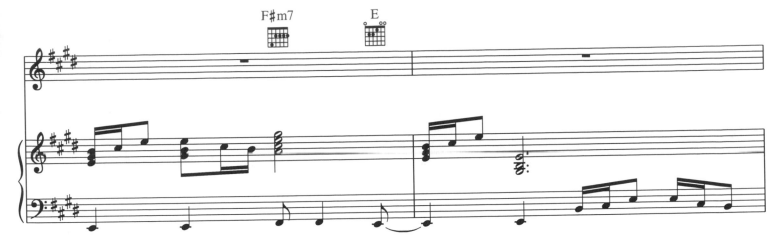

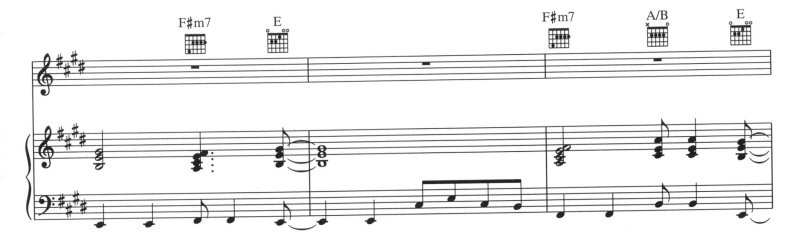

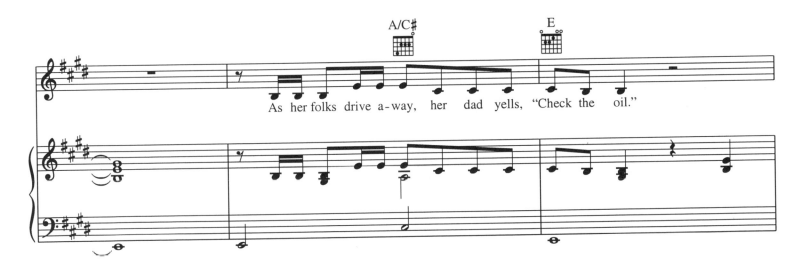

As her folks drive a-way, her dad yells, "Check the oil."

Mom stares out the win-dow and says, "I'm leav-in' my girl." She said, "It

did-n't seem like that long a - go" when she stood _ there and let her own

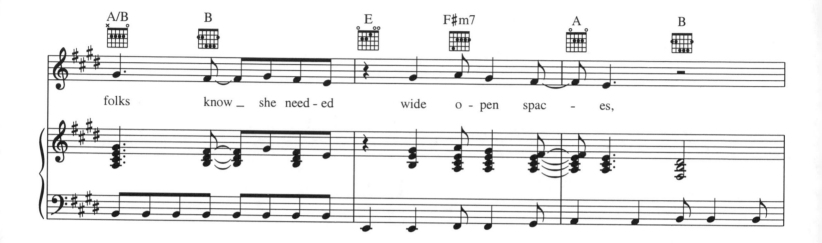

folks know _ she need - ed wide o - pen spac - es,

room to make _ her big __ mis - takes. She needs _

new _____ fac - es. She knows the high

stakes. __ She knows the high stakes, __ she knows the high _____ stakes.. Wide o - pen spac -

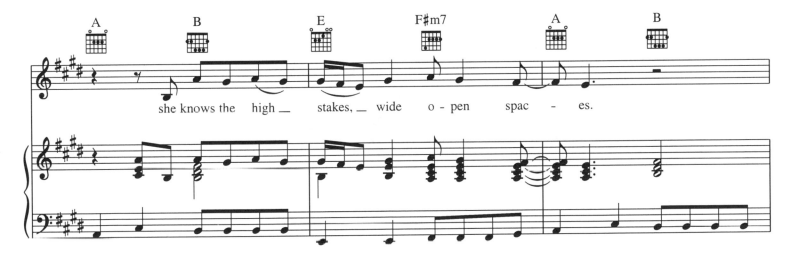

- es, she knows the high ___ stakes,

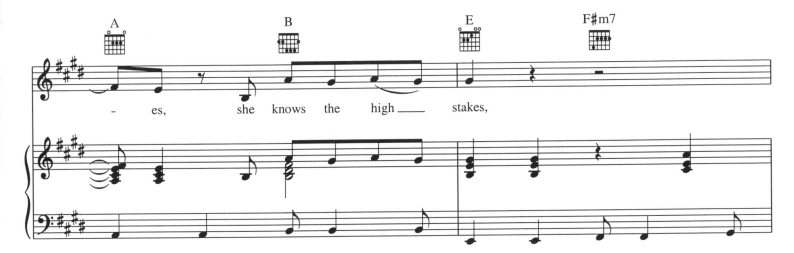

she knows the high __ stakes, __ wide o - pen spac - es.

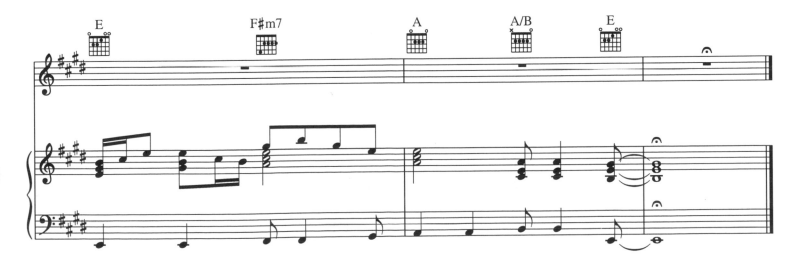

YOU ARE MY SUNSHINE

Words and Music by JIMMIE DAVIS
and CHARLES MITCHELL

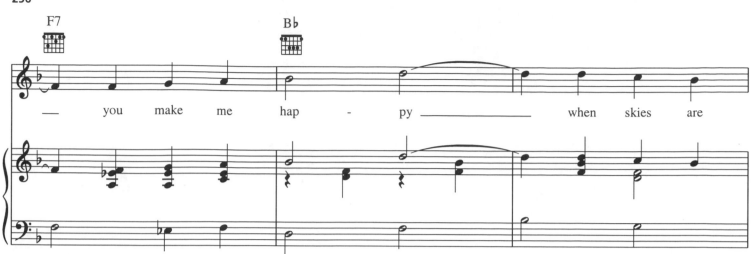

you make me hap - py _____ when skies are

gray. _____ You'll nev - er know, dear, _____ how much I

love you; _____ Please don't take my sun - shine a -

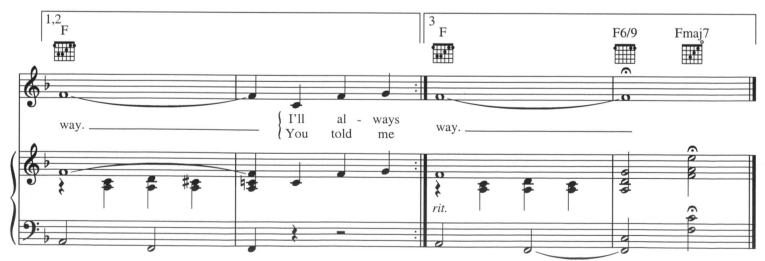

way. _____
I'll al - ways
You told me
way. _____

YOU LOOK SO GOOD IN LOVE

Words and Music by KERRY CHATER,
RORY BOURKE and GLEN BALLARD

An Easy 3

Oh how you spar - kle, and oh how you shine, ___
He how must you have stol - en some stars how from you the

sky ___ that flush on ___ them your cheeks is
and gave to you to

YOU NEEDED ME

Words and Music by
RANDY GOODRUM

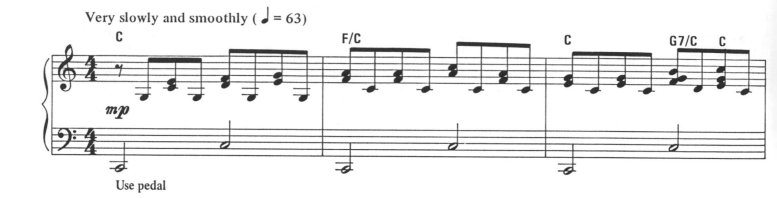

I cried a tear, you wiped it dry. I was con-

-fused, you cleared my mind. I sold my soul, you bought it

back for me,___ and held it up and gave it dig- ni- ty.___ Some-how you

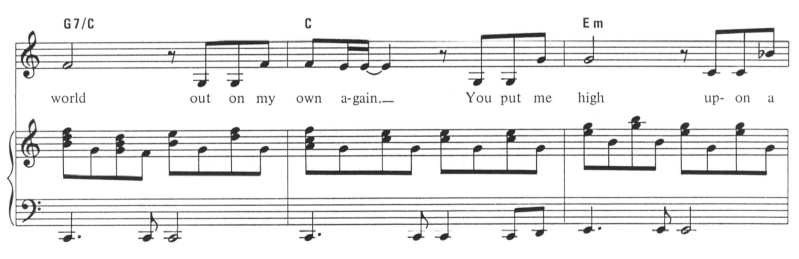

need- ed me. You gave me strength to stand a- lone a- gain,___ to face the

world out on my own a- gain.___ You put me high up- on a

ped- es- tal,___ so high that I___ can al- most see___ e- ter- ni- ty.___ You

hand   when it was cold.   When I was lost   you took me

home.   You gave me hope,   when I was at the end,—   and turned my

lies   back in- to truth a-gain.—   You e- ven

called me friend.   You gave me strength   to stand a- lone a-gain,—   to face the

YOUR CHEATIN' HEART

Words and Music by
HANK WILLIAMS

Moderately

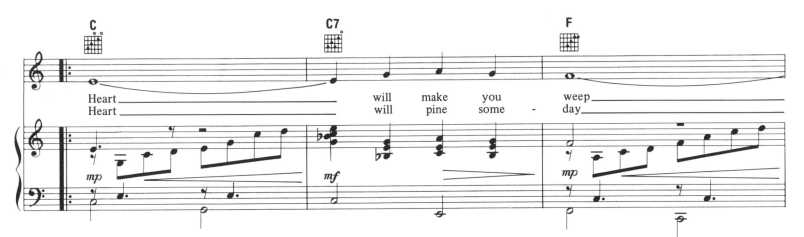

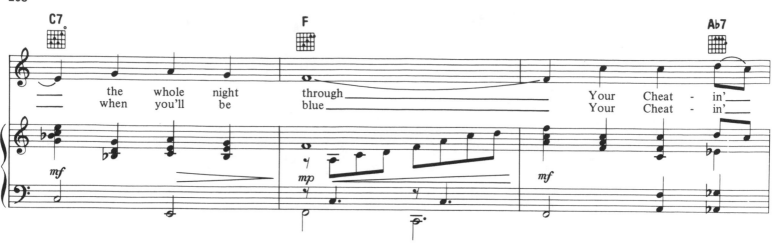

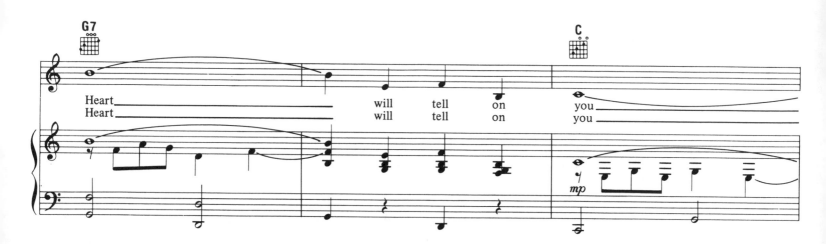

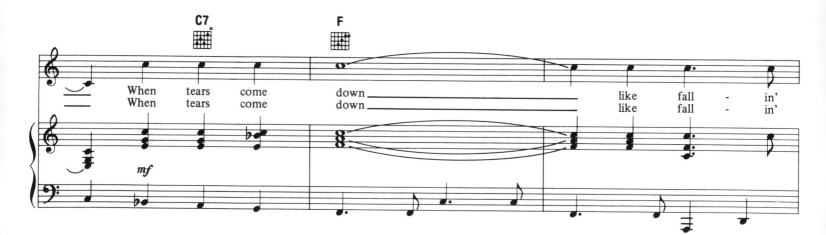

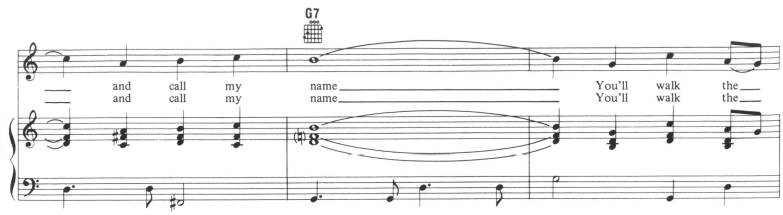

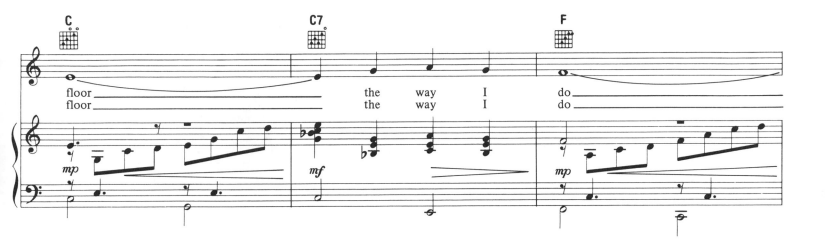

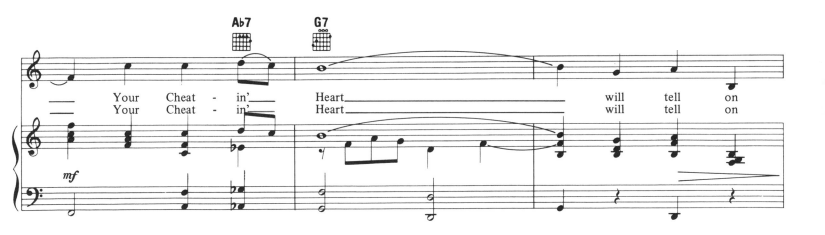

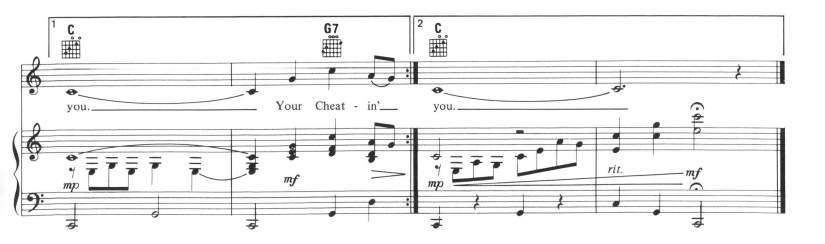

Contemporary & Classic Country

More great country hits from Hal Leonard arranged for piano and voice with guitar chords.

#1 Country Hits Of The Nineties
24 hot favorites, including: Achy Breaky Heart • Alibis • Boot Scootin' Boogie • Friends in Low Places • Hard Rock Bottom of Your Heart • It Matters to Me • Wide Open Spaces • and more.
00311699 ....$10.95

Hot Country Dancin'
Over 30 toe-tapping, boot-scootin' favorites guaranteed to get you dancing! Includes: Achy Breaky Heart • Friends In Low Places • Here's A Quarter (Call Someone Who Cares) • Hey, Good Lookin' • I Feel Lucky • and more.
00311621 ....$12.95

Country Inspiration
21 sentimental favorites, including: Brotherly Love • Guardian Angels • I Saw the Light • Love Can Build a Bridge • Love Without End, Amen • The Vows Go Unbroken • Why Me Lord? • and more.
00311616 ....$10.95

51 Country Standards
A collection of 51 of country's biggest hits, including: (Hey Won't You Play) Another Somebody Done Somebody Wrong Song • By the Time I Get to Phoenix • Could I Have This Dance • Daddy Sang Bass • Forever and Ever, Amen • God Bless the U.S.A. • Green Green Grass of Home • Islands in the Stream • King of the Road • Little Green Apples • Lucille • Mammas Don't Let Your Babies Grow Up to Be Cowboys • Ruby Don't Take Your Love to Town • Stand by Me • Through the Years • Your Cheatin' Heart.
00359517 ....$14.95

The Award-Winning Songs Of The Country Music Association – 1984-1996
40 country award-winners, including: Achy Breaky Heart • Ain't That Lonely Yet • Baby's Got Her Blue Jeans On • Boot Scootin' Boogie • Daddy's Hands • Down at the Twist and Shout • Forever and Ever, Amen • Friends in Low Places • God Bless the U.S.A. • I Swear • The Keeper of the Stars • Where've You Been • and more. Also includes a photo library of the winners.
00313081 ....$17.95

The Branson Songbook
As one of the most popular vacation destinations in the U.S. and more live music per mile than even Nashville, Branson, Missouri, has now become the new music mecca for more than 5 million tourists annually. This book celebrates the music and artists of this hot new spot with 19 songs, including: Moon River • Blue Velvet • Gentle on My Mind • Bubbles in the Wine • Yesterday When I Was Young • and many more. Also includes an introduction with photos.
00311693 ....$12.95

100 Most Wanted
Highlights: A Boy Named Sue • Break It to Me Gently • Crying My Heart out over You • Heartbroke • I.O.U. • I Know a Heartache When I See One • Mammas Don't Let Your Babies Grow Up to Be Cowboys • My Heroes Have Always Been Cowboys • Stand by Me • Save the Last Dance for Me • You're the First Time I've Thought About Leaving • You're the Reason God Made Oklahoma • many more.
00360730 ....$15.95

Cheatin' And Drinkin' Songs
47 country crooning classics, including: Daytime Friends • Don't The Girls All Get Prettier At Closin' Time • Friends In Low Places • I'm Gonna Hire A Wino To Decorate Our Home • Papa Loved Mama • Ruby, Don't Take Your Love To Town • Straight Tequila Night • The Whiskey Ain't Workin' • Your Cheatin' Heart • and more.
00311618 ....$14.95

The Best Contemporary Country Ballads
30 heart-felt hits, including: After All This Time • Alibis • The Greatest Man I Never Knew • I Can Love You Like That • I Meant Every Word He Said • I Want to Be Loved Like That • If Tomorrow Never Comes • One Boy, One Girl • When You Say Nothing at All • Where've You Been • more.
00310116 ....$14.95

90's Country Gold
29 chartburners, including: Achy Breaky Heart • Boot Scootin' Boogie • Down at the Twist and Shout • Friends in Low Places • I Feel Lucky • Neon Moon • Shameless • She Is His Only Need • Straight Tequila Night • and more.
00311607 ....$12.95

Country Love Songs
34 songs featuring: Butterfly Kisses • Check Yes or No • For the Good Times • I Never Knew Love • Love Can Build a Bridge • The Vows Go Unbroken (Always True to You) • and more.
00311528 ....$12.95

Country Women of the 90s
25 hits from today's hottest stars. Songs include: Down at the Twist and Shout • The Greatest Man I Never Knew • I Feel Lucky • Maybe It Was Memphis • No One Else on Earth • Rumor Has It • Time Passes By • Where've You Been • The Woman Before Me • and more.
00311605 ....$10.95

FOR MORE INFORMATION, SEE YOUR LOCAL MUSIC DEALER, OR WRITE TO:

HAL•LEONARD® CORPORATION

7777 W. BLUEMOUND RD. P.O. BOX 13819 MILWAUKEE, WI 53213

Prices, contents, and availability subject to change without notice.

0399